FASTTRACK
COACHING

WITH A FOREWORD BY MICHAEL J. RICE

FastTrack
Coaching

For Building a
21st Century
Financial Practice

Matt Oechsli

Total Achievement Publishing
P.O. Box 29385
Greensboro, NC 27429

Designed and typeset by WMB Design – Greensboro, NC

Cover design by Foster & Foster, Inc. – Fairfield, IA

Printed in the United States of America

ISBN: 0-9656765-1-X

FOREWORD

During recent years, the paramount goal of most companies in our industry has been to deliver a variety of financial services to the greatest number of people in the most profitable manner. Today, that goal is being redefined by significant obstacles and shifts in our marketplace that have become ongoing topics of conversation throughout our Firm, as well as the industry. As both the market and the client segments become more clearly defined, it is necessary to continually reevaluate our Firm's position and ensure that it is aligned with our strategy.

Affluent investors are searching for solutions dealing with the multidimensional aspects of their finances and we at Prudential Financial are working hard to fill this need. Our *Growing and Protecting Your Wealth* tag line is applicable to the multiple client segments of the investment and insurance arenas. We continue to integrate our selected line of financial services to make that achievable for each client.

Changes in strategy require changes in tactical implementation. Those changes, either subtle or dramatic, are needed to accelerate the rate of attracting affluent assets, improving our professionalism in delivering advice, and enhancing our client's experience with Prudential Financial. Our most pressing task is to make certain that our Financial Advisors and Branch support can successfully implement these changes at the Branch Office. Tactical excellence is what makes strategic decisions successful.

Thorough training helps, but even the greatest training does not fully accompany the individual back to the office, to help him or her gain the additional insight and confidence required to apply what has been taught. It takes a manager who is skilled in coaching to provide the guidance, feedback, and accountability that is necessary to accelerate the performance improvement process. Fortunately, the skill of coaching can be learned and improved upon for those who have not yet successfully acquired it.

Matt Oechsli's *FastTrack Coaching* is a tool that, when applied properly, can help transform managers into true performance coaches. The more skilled our managers are at coaching, the more effectively our financial professionals can deliver the Client Advisory Process to serve our clients, essentially the mass affluent and affluent.

There are a number of factors that make *FastTrack Coaching* a valuable supplement to the Financial Advisor Business System and Branch Business System at this particular time:

- It applies the performance coaching process to the specific challenges we face as we seek to attract, service, and retain affluent clients.

- Both individual and team coaching are addressed; and the section on Achiever Groups provides a unique working partnership approach to impacting performance improvement.

- The chapters covering the psychology of individual performance and the dynamics of teams provide helpful hints for understanding how to focus and accelerate performance improvement.

- The author, Matt Oechsli, is well known for his coaching skills. With more than 20 years of experience in our industry, he has worked closely with Prudential Financial for the past 10 years.

Attaining the skill of coaching is only the first step in becoming an indispensable manager; it must then be practiced, maintained and mastered. Now, more than ever, Financial Advisors need motivation, guidance and direction. Matt Oechsli's *FastTrack Coaching* is an excellent tool that can be used to build and enhance relationships, especially during a transformation process, which is why I am placing it in your hands – the hands of those whom I believe will take full advantage of its potential.

Michael J. Rice
Executive Director – Retail Branch Group
Prudential Securities

Prudential Securities is a Prudential Financial company

CONTENTS

INTRODUCTION

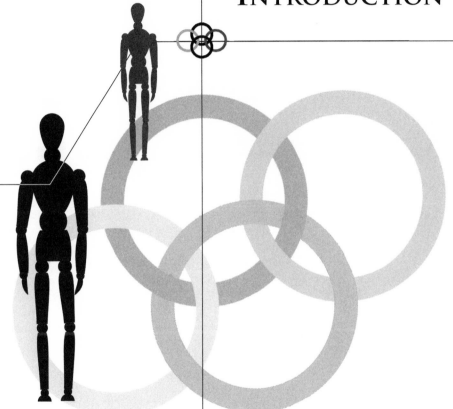

The secret of success of every man who has ever been successful lies in the fact that he formed the habit of doing things that failures don't like to do.

ALBERT E. N. GRAY

Introduction

I love Albert Gray's quote. It was the heart of a speech he delivered at the 1940 National Association of Life Underwriters convention in Philadelphia, and it has become a timeless nugget of undeniable truth. Any success I've had with coaching financial professionals over the past 20 years has come from helping them apply that principle each and every day.

It is no secret that financial advisors need a habit adjustment if they want to develop a sustainable fee-based practice that caters to upper-middle class and affluent investors. Everywhere financial advisors turn someone is encouraging, pushing, or directing them to build a 21st century financial practice targeting upper-middle class and affluent investors. They are being told that in spite of dot-com failures, unprecedented business and accounting scandals, client portfolio losses, and the unpredictability of financial markets, this is the greatest opportunity the financial services industry has ever seen.

On an intellectual level everyone agrees, but on an emotional level too many financial advisors are stuck. A few of the best and brightest do know what to do, are doing it, and are being handsomely rewarded for their efforts. We have the privilege of supporting several in this elite group; a group that does not have a lot of competition because so many financial advisors are paralyzed.

The logical move for financial advisors who are stuck is to turn to their manager for help. I've worked with many veteran managers over the years who were highly disciplined, ran tight ships, understood the business, passed their audits, conducted effective sales meetings, and were able to drive their firm's initiatives when necessary. But only a few were schooled in coaching techniques that enabled them to help financial advisors navigate the daily challenges while simultaneously capitalizing on new opportunities.

The premise of this book is simple. In light of the unique set of opportunities and challenges confronting the 21st century financial advisor, performance coaching is essential and has become a vital challenge every manager needs to master. I keep hearing the cynical comment that "people don't change." That is rubbish! Many financial advisors may not like to change, but they will when the following three factors are in place:

1. **They have a good reason to change**. And now they have that reason! No one is denying the reality of the high net worth client opportunity.

2. **They know what to do and how to do it**. There are programs like ours that will help, but that's not enough when the performance gap is so wide.

3. **The right support system is in place to help make the necessary changes**. In order to capitalize on today's opportunities; programs, new products, and training will help – but they rarely have sustaining impact without the "right" support.

Performance coaching is the right support. A skilled coach will help financial advisors set the right goals, apply programs and training the right way, define the right activities to move them step-by-step toward those goals, and provide the right kind of support to keep them on track.

This is not a book we were seeking to write. But after looking for sources that we could recommend to our clients and receiving inquiries about equipping managers to coach performance, we finally concluded that the available books are too general and conceptual to provide the help needed in this challenging financial services environment. Creating the kind of book we believe will be useful has been a challenging, but valuable and rewarding endeavor.

This book is targeted toward managers of financial professionals in every corner of the industry, whether it is investments, insurance, banking, accounting, or financial planning. We use the term "financial advisor" throughout, but the focus is on any financial professional who is looking to attract and service an upper-middle class and affluent clientele.

You will find knowledge, processes and techniques in this book, that are necessary to develop the skills required to successfully coach financial advisors and wealth management teams in the 21st century. The coaching steps and action agreements are designed to accelerate performance improvement, not drag it out ad nauseam. FastTrack Coaching is more than a title; it can actually be a reality.

Challenging opportunities do not need to be out of reach for the 21st century financial advisor or wealth management team. Performance gaps can be closed. Change can take place within your financial advisor corps. This book is written to show you how to help others form "the habit of doing things that failures don't like to do."

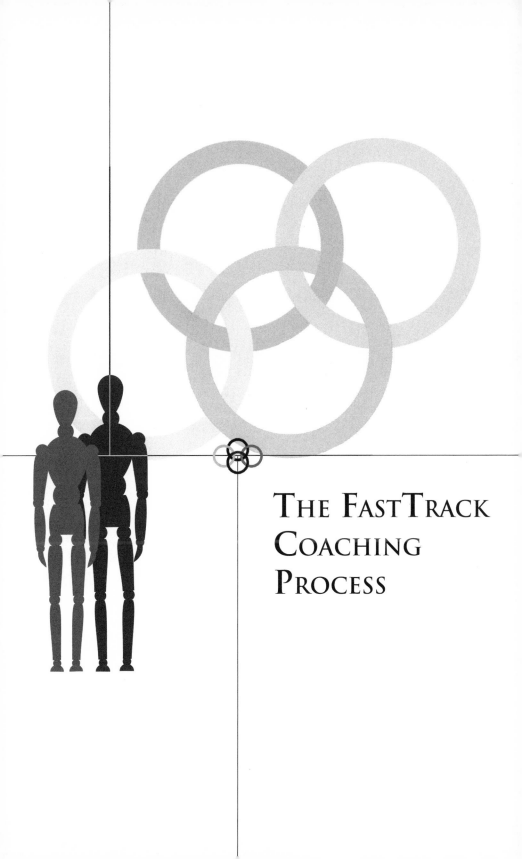

THE FASTTRACK
COACHING
PROCESS

CHAPTER 1

HOW TO BECOME
AN INDISPENSABLE
MANAGER

Coaches who can outline plays on a blackboard are a dime a dozen. The ones who win get inside their players and motivate.

VINCE LOMBARDI

Attracting resources and putting them to work is only the beginning. The task of a business is to make resources productive.

PETER DRUCKER

The opportunity to advise the affluent in the management of their wealth is inarguably the greatest opportunity to ever present itself in the world of financial services. So much so that it has created a crisis in the retail side of the financial services industry.

Financial advisors are being challenged to change, to transition from the old one-dimensional sales and marketing model of Wall Street to a multidimensional solutions-based approach. In effect, financial advisors are being forced to "raise their game" if they intend to capitalize on the opportunities presented by the affluent. They have also discovered that they do not possess all the expertise required to provide multidimensional solutions to the affluent. More often than not, providing financial solutions requires a team approach.

Change is easier said than done. Some financial advisors don't know what to do. Others know, but are intimidated by the challenge. Behavioral and attitudinal habits developed over the years are holding back many financial advisors. A few are successfully making the transition, but many are not. They seem to be paralyzed by uncertainty and are unable to do what is required to successfully attract, service, and retain affluent investors.

We at The Oechsli Institute have been conducting studies of successful financial advisors, wealth management teams, and affluent investors for the past three years. Those studies have continually reinforced four critical findings:

1. Affluent investors are searching for a solutions provider who can service all the multidimensional aspects of their personal finances.

2. Significant gaps exist between what affluent investors expect and what they perceive they are receiving from their financial advisors.

3. Many financial advisors are struggling to make the changes necessary to close these gaps and are searching for help.

4. Programs and training alone cannot provide the help needed. Managers who understand and apply the art of performance coaching are desperately needed.

It is clear from our research, as well as the studies of others, that few managers have mastered the art of performance coaching. Those who have are indispensable.

Having coached financial advisors for more than 20 years, I am keenly aware of the benefits that can be gained from a coaching relationship. A coach becomes a personal guide who helps financial advisors bridge the gap between where they are right now, and where they want to go. A skilled coach will help a financial advisor to stay on track, to remain focused on the tasks at hand, to prioritize what really matters, and to gain improved clarity. A skilled coach will help financial advisors discover and apply new ideas and approaches that expand their comfort zones. Working with a coach provides an accountability mechanism that enables a financial advisor to think bigger, take quicker action, and do a more effective job than could possibly be accomplished working alone. A skilled performance coach is truly a financial advisor's FastTrack to success.

Currently much of our work at The Oechsli Institute involves educating, coaching, and developing tools to assist financial advisors in making the transition to a 21st Century Financial Practice™†. We are confident that with the right type of coaching, a significant percentage of financial advisors can successfully make this transition within 18 to 24 months. However, we are not Pollyannaish in our thinking. We are acutely aware of the challenges involved.

This FastTrack Coaching process is designed to address both the urgency and the opportunity in this challenge. The purpose of this book is to pro-

† 21st Century Financial Practice is a phrase used throughout this book. It is a term that defines the program developed by The Oechsli Institute for transforming transaction based providers into solutions based wealth management teams, equipped to meet the multidimensional needs of the affluent. Details regarding the program and accompanying products are available at the following web site: www.oechsli.com or by phone at 800-883-6582.

vide a practical guide that will help managers coach financial advisors and wealth management teams in making the necessary changes to success-fully attract, service, and retain the loyalty of affluent investors.

ACCORDING TO OUR RESEARCH

Our initial effort to define the challenges relating to the affluent market segment began in the waning months of the 20th century, when we sur-veyed a random sample of affluent investors. Our focus was on those who used a financial advisor to assist them in making investment deci-sions beyond employer provided retirement and investment programs. The results from our research were startling. With a 95.2 percent valida-tion factor, survey respondents reported that their financial advisor was not meeting their expectations in 14 of the 20 qualities they rated as being most important. Of those 14 qualities, nine showed enough statisti-cal significance to indicate an alarming gap between advisor performance and client expectations. The four largest performance expectation gaps illustrate the seriousness of the challenge facing your financial advisors. Essentially, affluent investors complained,

- I do not receive satisfactory value for the fees and/or commissions I pay.

- I do not trust the quality of the financial advice I receive.

- I do not trust that the financial advice I receive is always in my best interest.

- I do not always receive a follow-through on promises made.

To better understand these and other issues, we conducted another study in the fall of 2000. We targeted a group considered to be success-ful ($600,000+) financial advisors. We had two basic objectives: 1) Learn more about the efforts made by, and the needs of, financial advisors in terms of attracting and maintaining the loyalty of affluent clients and 2) Measure the financial advisors' perception of the support provided by their managers.

From a sampling of 2,700 financial advisors, we discovered (with *95.2 percent* confidence) several interesting facts. Although *93 percent* stated that they were targeting affluent investors,

- *Forty-nine percent* admitted that they had lost affluent investors to the competition over the past 12 months.

- *Seventy-seven percent* did not have a complete, written long-range business plan that went beyond production goals.

- *Eighty-six percent* did not have strict minimum guidelines for opening an account. Those who did have minimum guidelines, reported a median guideline of $100,000 in investable assets.

- *Seventy percent* had more than 300 households in their book of business.

In the third quarter of 2001, we surveyed 200 wealth management teams of which *65 percent* reported that at least half of their client base fit the affluent client category (defined as a $500,000 minimum investable asset account). Although several of our findings resembled earlier studies, a number of specifics grabbed our attention,

- Only *32 percent* required a $500,000 minimum in investable assets for new accounts.

- *Thirty-six percent* had a written long-range business plan beyond production quotas, and only *30 percent* had an ideal client profile to guide their marketing efforts.

- *Eleven percent* had a metrics system to monitor individual and team performance.

- *Twenty-two percent* provided a wide range of wealth management solutions.

We also found that...

- *Seventy-eight percent* said they were currently part of a wealth management team, but only *25 percent* said they had clearly delegated areas of responsibility for team members. Which was interesting since all referred to themselves as a wealth management team.

- *Sixty-eight percent* said their marketing strategy was based on building client loyalty, but only *three percent* had specific criteria they used to measure each client's loyalty behavior.

Our research continually indicates that components vital to the development of a successful 21st Century Financial Practice are missing. Even those financial advisors making an earnest effort to implement the transition are ignoring many critical elements. They're on a "slow track" to somewhere; but the question is, where?

Everyone appears to be targeting affluent investors. But what is being done to help financial advisors and teams develop the additional knowledge required to provide multidimensional financial solutions to their affluent clients? What is being done to assist them in developing the new patterns of behavior necessary to serve this market niche? It takes goal focus, professional self-discipline, and willingness to step outside one's comfort zone to forge ahead and travel the FastTrack to 21st century success. We asked our most recent group of 200 teams about these very qualities, and here is what they told us:

- *Five percent* said they were highly goal focused.

- *Thirteen percent* said they were professionally very self-disciplined.

- *Nineteen percent* said they consistently step outside their comfort zone to pursue business opportunities.

These low percentages suggest that the majority of the financial advisors are still operating a sales practice, which is exactly what affluent investors do not want. Whether it is due to unwillingness, ignorance, or inability to do what is necessary to attract and build the loyalty of affluent clients; opportunities are being lost.

Don't give up. Don't ever give up.

Jim Valvano

The Cry for Help

Our questions in the fall 2000 survey also addressed branch management. We wanted to better understand how financial advisors view the role their managers play in supporting their quest to work with affluent clients. The best indicator of that support is its impact on the financial advisor's loyalty to the firm, earned primarily through the attitudes and efforts of the branch manager.

We learned that several managerial support factors impact the financial advisors' willingness to continue to conduct business through his or her current firm, to consider new products and tools recommended by their firm, to resist business opportunities with other firms, and to provide referrals of other financial advisors to their firm. Those managerial support factors are listed below:

- **Trust** – Trusting the manager to give advice that is in the financial advisor's best interest.

- **Help** – Receiving the manager's help with developing, reviewing, and making necessary adjustments to the advisor's business plan.

- **Support** – Receiving the manager's help with maintaining a good level of personal health. The need for a supported sense of well-being was especially strong.

The message is clear. Financial advisors feel the pressure to change how they conduct their business. Their eyes are focused on investors with higher incomes and net worth – people who resist the traditional sales approach. They realize that gaining and maintaining client loyalty is essential and requires a long-range business plan, an ideal client profile, networking amongst affluent centers-of-influence, new attraction methods, a wider range of financial solutions, a highly effective financial advisory process, and a wealth management team that provides Ritz-Carlton level service with FedEx efficiency.

However, making this transition will not happen if the manager simply gives them a slap on the back and a "go get 'em Harry" motivational speech. Nor will it occur with simply being told what to do, or even as the result of classroom training. Instead, a successful transition will require the right type, amount, and timing of performance coaching by managers who are in the field. Financial advisors and wealth management teams need a manager who is there to share both the disappointments and successes, someone who has developed a personal relationship with them and who knows how to support their efforts to accomplish the necessary tasks that lead to goal achievement.

Lack of goal achievement is often the result of not knowing how to get there, or not understanding why it's important to make the effort. That is not the case here. When an individual or team elects to target the affluent through building a 21st Century Financial Practice, both the end and the means are well defined, as illustrated below.

Goal: Build a 21st Century Financial Practice that enables me to successfully attract, service, and retain the loyalty of affluent clients.

Means: Complete the 14 Strategic Thinking Exercises and apply the 11 Tactical How-To's as I work my way through the Business Development, Financial Advisory, Operational Efficiency, and Client Loyalty processes and build a competent Wealth Management Team.

As helpful as it is for financial advisors to know where they want to go, the gap between where they are now and what they envision for their future can seem overwhelming.

For the financial advisor, success is often an "if only" proposition.

If I start listening to everyone talk about all the changes we need to make and begin looking through the materials provided by my firm, I feel overwhelmed. As I consider the new knowledge and skills I will have to develop in the process, doubts begin to creep in and I feel overwhelmed. I wonder about my ability to pull it off.

But...

If only I could be guided by someone who knows how I feel and could collaborate with me in my transition; who could help me stay focused, answer my "stupid" questions, quiet my fears, and would encourage me to keep doing what I need to do even when I'd rather not do it - that would really help!

If only my manager understood the steps I have to take and could help me organize them sensibly, that would help. If my manager could help me identify and overcome the obstacles along the way; that would be even better. If I knew that someone with knowledge and authority would support me, I would be willing to step outside my comfort zone and go for it!

This is the financial advisor's cry for help. The specific words you hear might differ, but the call is the same — and urgent. That is why any branch manager who learns and applies the art of FastTrack performance coaching will quickly become indispensable. Firms where branch managers have mastered the art of coaching will quickly become the place of choice for financial advisors and teams trying to build a 21st Century Financial Practice.

In-house certification through classroom training is not enough. Although training provides exposure to the elements involved in making the transition to a 21st Century Financial Practice, training does not give financial advisors the confidence and skills to break out of their comfort zone and FastTrack their way to success. Coaching, done properly, is the best solution. For many, it's the only solution.

Much has been written in the sporting world about the relationship that golfer extraordinaire Tiger Woods has with his coach. Yet few people understand what's involved. Tiger, already an exceptional golfer, simply wanted to raise the bar and knew he couldn't raise it by himself. He needed the assistance of a skilled golf coach. If I want to understand myself better, I go to a counselor. When I want to improve my recreational tennis game, I find a coach. Webster says to coach means "to instruct, direct, or prompt." Coaching involves taking action in order to create action on the part of someone else. The direction is always forward, aimed toward a meaningful goal.

We know what we are. We know not what we may be.

WILLIAM SHAKESPEARE

FastTrack Coaching Defined

The term "coaching" has taken on a life of its own in the 21st century, but simply changing the name of a training program to a "coaches clinic" does not mean performance coaching is taking place. To make certain we are thinking in the same terms, here is our working definition.

FastTrack Coaching is a collaborative process
between coach and financial advisor,
designed to focus and accelerate
personal and professional development.

The stronger the collaborative relationship between financial advisor and coach, the more accelerated the development becomes. Put yourself in the place of the person being coached for a moment. Imagine that I, as coach, am privy to your dreams and aspirations. I know how you think, what makes you tick, what you value above all else; your passions. I am keenly aware of your strengths and weaknesses. Armed with this understanding, I am in a much stronger position to help you clarify your goals, develop action steps, determine the tools you need, and guide you step-by-step toward reaching your goals. No trainer in front of a classroom can come close to that.

But, to successfully coach financial advisors and teams to establish their 21st Century Financial Practice within 18 to 24 months, you will need more than a definition. You need to expand your knowledge and skill in the following four key areas:

1. **The FastTrack Coaching Process** – In Chapter 2, you will discover there are significant differences between coaching and managing. Coaching must be understood as a process; not a series of events, but an ongoing process that has a well-defined beginning and end. How you begin a coaching relationship is critical. Initiating a coaching relationship is the focus of Chapter 3. In Chapter 4, you will learn how to create a 5-step FastTrack Action Agreement to help those you coach define what needs to be done and determine how you will support their efforts. These actions are what make the FastTrack concept become reality. Finally in Chapter 5, you will be introduced to 14 FastTrack Action Agreement outlines that you can use to coach individuals and teams through the four processes that are essential for targeting affluent investors: 1) building their business, 2) providing financial advisory services, 3) establishing operational efficiency, and 4) building client loyalty.

2. **Coaching Individuals** – In the second section of the book, you will be introduced to the Psychology of Performance. It is essential for a

performance coach to possess a strong working knowledge of how the mind works and how new habits are developed to replace old ones, and that is the focus of Chapter 6. How goals impact motivation is covered in Chapter 7. How to skillfully apply the Achievement Cycle to the coaching process is the subject of Chapter 8. The understanding you gain from this section will help create many of the "aha's" that will occur throughout your coaching experience.

3. **Coaching Teams** – The emphasis on teams in today's world of financial services exists for a reason, and you will discover the answer to "Why teams?" in Chapter 9. Different levels of teams exist today, but only Level 4 Teams can adequately serve the needs of affluent clients. Coaching teams through the four stages of development is the focus of Chapter 10. You will also find a list of critical factors that can make or break any wealth management team you coach. We call these critical factors the 12 Commandments of Successful Teams. A wealth management team is formed specifically to attract, service, and retain the loyalty of affluent clients and is a unique brand of team. It is critical to create the right team structure and establish the right compensation agreement and both of these concepts will be covered in Chapter 11.

4. **Facilitating Achiever Groups** – No, this is not simply an extension of coaching teams. The Achiever Group concept can be applied to a number of situations. The groups could be financial advisors who need to develop prospecting skills; operations or support people who need to become more efficient; technical people who need to manage projects better; team leaders who need to handle group dynamics; or even managers who need to learn how to coach. Achiever Groups meet six times. Between those meetings, participants continue the accountability and support processes in working partner teams. The Achiever Group concept is introduced in Chapter 12. You will learn how to facilitate an achiever group meeting in Chapter 13 and Chapter 14 describes the achiever group experience from a coach's perspective.

We believe we have created a complete and comprehensive approach to performance coaching applied specifically to building a 21st Century Financial Practice and wealth management team. It is directed primarily toward the branch manager and is certain to help make any branch manager indispensable – today and in the future.

Your FastTrack Coaching Checklist

All of this is easy to write about and fairly simple to discuss. However, becoming a competent coach requires commitment at a very basic level. Coaching is a hands-on process, not a one-time event. It demands that you be in the trenches with those being coached, feeling their fears, experiencing their pain, and sharing the successes of every individual, even when you are coaching a team. You will learn to coach primarily by coaching.

However, it does help to be prepared. If you are feeling a bit inadequate for the job, don't be discouraged. Our intention is to use this book as a medium that will take you step-by-step through everything you need to gain the necessary knowledge and develop the requisite skills. We also recognize that time is one of your most precious commodities and have made every effort to make the FastTrack Coaching process extremely time efficient. In fact, if done properly, it will save you time.

Here is a checklist for you to think through as you prepare to embark on your FastTrack Coaching journey.

☑ **Be convinced that coaching is important, and then make a personal commitment to become the best coach you can possibly be.**

You can forget about half-hearted attempts at coaching performance. The financial advisors you want to impact will see through your efforts and think less of you than if you had never attempted a coaching relationship in the first place. This is as basic as not promising a child something, whether it's a bedtime story or a new computer, unless you are committed to follow through. Recognizing the need for performance coaching is the first step. Committing the time to actually perform the necessary activities is next. Our research tells us clearly — the most important activity any manager could perform is performance coaching.

☑ **Sharpen your interpersonal skills.**

Most managers know how to work with people, but gaining a good working knowledge of how to deliver feedback is crucial for the coach. A performance coach must be experienced in the art of holding people accountable and yet needs to provide ongoing support, free of any ambiguities. And remember, telling is not coaching. You will find Section Two, Coaching Individuals, very useful for fine-tuning these interpersonal skills.

☑ **Develop a passion for learning**

Since performance coaching is a process rather than an event, it is always evolving and never becomes stagnant. A performance coach must make a commitment to life-long learning.

As you begin to implement the FastTrack Coaching process, and as we guide you through the chapters of this book, you will be coaching individuals and teams who are attempting to develop a 21st Century Financial Practice, which is a business model we built from the research discussed earlier. Yet the world of financial services is changing so rapidly that another model might eventually evolve with its accompanying learning requirements. That means that you must continue to be a student of human behavior, team dynamics, and the financial services industry. As you learn the art of performance coaching, be assured that the knowledge and skills you gain will transcend any changes in the industry that you can imagine.

If you are ready to learn and are prepared to consistently do what the "average" manager-trainer-coach will not do, it's time to move on to find out what the FastTrack Coaching Process is all about.

CHAPTER 2

MAKING THE TRANSITION FROM MANAGER TO COACH

Styles of coaching may differ - from bombastic to philosophical. But at the end of the day, any good coach is a teacher.

MARV LEVY

I believe the true road to preeminent success in any line is to make yourself a master of that line.

ANDREW CARNEGIE

In Chapter 1, we talked about the transition a financial advisor must go through in order to build a successful 21st Century Financial Practice. There is also a transition that most managers must experience in their efforts to become an effective coach.

I suspect that you have encountered the following statement, or at least some variation: "What we need today are leaders, not managers." A leader is a person who can visualize opportunities for success and articulate that vision so well that others want to follow, be involved, and help make it a reality. Building a 21st Century Financial Practice that successfully attracts, services, and retains affluent clients is today's big opportunity for financial advisors. Helping others envision a believable future is where effective coaching begins. But before they accept you as their coach, your financial advisors must first seek your leadership.

Another aspect of the transition from manager to coach focuses on how you will work with your financial advisors to achieve a 21st Century Financial Practice. The wider the gap between where they are now and where they need to go, the more critical coaching becomes. In order to sustain an 18 to 24 month effort, the individuals and teams you coach must find their own reasons to stay with it. FastTrack Coaching is uniquely suited for that type of situation, but it will not happen without a plan.

Jerry, a veteran branch manager of a complex with over 70 financial advisors, was convinced that if he could persuade one of his largest producers into a coaching relationship, his transition from manager to coach would be seventy-five percent complete. Doing his homework, Jerry and his operations manager analyzed every household (the number of positions, fees versus commissions, dead assets, number and quality of new relationships over the past 12 months, opportunities) that comprised this large financial advisor's book of business.

Rather than discuss his findings with his financial advisor and run the risk of a defensive reaction, Jerry simply printed a detailed report, organized it in a 3-ring binder and highlighted three critical areas that warranted attention. He then left the report on the financial advisor's desk one evening.

At 7:30 a.m. the following morning, this successful financial advisor and Jerry were engaged in an intense discussion. The context of the discussion was "how-to" take his current business to the next level. It was the first time such a conversation took place between the two. Jerry's transition from manager to coach had just begun.

The transition from manager to coach is a fluid process. When you enter into a coaching relationship, you will find yourself segueing back and forth between your managerial role and your coaching role. In very general terms, coaching guides the process that enables others to produce the results they want to achieve.

Managers who become effective coaches learn how and when to move comfortably between their dual roles as manager and coach. Following are some examples of how the two roles compare.

MANAGER (FOCUS ON RESULTS)	COACH (FOCUS ON PROCESS)
Defines the required results.	Articulates future opportunities.
Directs and controls actions.	Empowers others to take action.
Motivates through fear of probable consequences.	Creates a safe, fearless environment conducive to risk taking.
Establishes deadlines.	Requires target dates and then clears the path.
Provides answers.	Asks questions and suggests options.
Solves problems.	Equips people to prevent and solve their own problems.
Approves.	Challenges and endorses.
Monitors current policies and procedures.	Encourages and facilitates change.

One of the terms that is used frequently in the context of coaching is *empowerment*. But what does that really mean? As the word suggests, it involves a shift of power and authority. When a manager empowers, he or she increases the individual's responsibility, authority, and flexibility in making day-to-day decisions. Although the term is only used once in the above contrast between manager and coach, it is implied in each transition. You truly empower the financial advisors and teams you coach when you,

- Help them see the possibilities before they set goals.

- Ask (not tell) them to do more than they have ever done before.

- Focus on their strengths, not just their weaknesses.

- Push them into doing, not just talking about it.

- Have them take full responsibility for everything.

- Help them re-frame what they are thinking or feeling.

- Help them learn from mistakes while maintaining their goal focus.

- Are unconditionally constructive in everything you say to them.

As you can see, coaching is a helping process that emerges from a rich professional relationship that you establish with others. In order to establish such a relationship, you will need to work hard at developing the following *capabilities*:

- **Awareness** – to diagnose accurately what is really going on, making certain that your own values and habits don't get in the way.

- **Empathy** – to identify with the other person's point of view and communicate that you do understand.

- **Listening** – to "hear" the problem or situation described without any pre-judging.

- **Flexibility** – to adjust to the work habits and desires of others.

- **Confidence** – to communicate high but realistic expectations for others, and to encourage them to learn from their experiences.

- **Probing** – to ask questions which clarify or extend their thinking.

- **Timing** – to question and offer information or suggestions at the exact moment that they are ready to hear and respond.

- **Synthesizing** – to see the interrelationships among pieces of information and be able to clearly explain those patterns.

- **Experimenting** – to encourage exploration and defer judgment when they actually do explore.

If you can only care enough for a result,
you will almost certainly attain it.

WILLIAM JAMES

We recognize that you, as both manager and coach, are faced with two realities each day: multiple responsibilities and limited time. Coaching is not a new management responsibility. It's an extension of, and actually a better approach to, one of the most important responsibilities you already have – equipping the financial advisors who report to you with the necessary tools and skills to improve their performance. We intend to help you do that, beginning with the ideas and information presented in this chapter.

However, coaching does require investing additional time and effort with each financial advisor and team you coach. Our goal is to help you make that investment wisely by targeting individuals and teams who have the greatest potential. That will be the subject of Chapter 3. By selecting carefully, you will discover that coaching enables both you and the financial advisors you coach to achieve considerably more in less time.

As a coach, you will go beyond what seems probable to make the improbable possible for those who seek your leadership and value you as their coach. The transition is a paradigm shift, attitudinally and behaviorally, for both financial advisor and manager. In Jerry's case, his large producer was not actively seeking Jerry's guidance at first. Like many successful financial advisors, he had seen managers come and go; and he operated under the old adage, "I don't expect my manager to help me, I just don't want him to hurt me."

But Jerry ventured far outside his comfort zone as manager to conduct a detailed analysis of the entire business of one of his largest financial advisors and compiled it in a 3-ring binder. Assuming the role of coach, Jerry went one step further and highlighted a few areas he thought could use immediate attention. This evaluation required more time than he would normally invest before meeting with one of his financial advisors, but it was time well spent. It took his larger producer completely by surprise and now their relationship has a new dimension; Jerry is now viewed as both manager and coach. This has impacted the working relationship Jerry has with his other financial advisors as well.

The benefits of this subtle transformation have been enormous for Jerry and for every financial advisor who now enters into a coaching relationship with him. When done right, coaching is truly the FastTrack to success.

CHAPTER 3

INITIATING A FASTTRACK COACHING RELATIONSHIP

The old adage 'People are your most important asset' is wrong. People are not your most important asset. The right people are.

JIM COLLINS

You cannot push anyone up a ladder unless he is willing to climb a little.

ANDREW CARNEGIE

FastTrack Coaching is serious business. It requires tackling some tough issues, asking delicate questions, conducting frank conversations, holding financial advisors accountable for taking a "walk on the wild side," venturing outside their comfort zone and doing what they need to do consistently.

The latest figures report that 80 percent of Americans are overweight. The result is a significant growth in the use of personal trainers. Training someone into good health and fitness is serious business. It requires commitment. Every good personal trainer has a set of criteria he or she uses to screen candidates. After all, they build their reputation by word-of-mouth, so it's important for them to increase their probability of success by selecting only those individuals who are committed enough to meet the criteria they have established.

The same rule of thumb applies to FastTrack Coaching. Garnered from over 20 years of performance coaching, and from more mistakes than I care to remember, I have developed a selection process you will find works quite well. The objective is to assist you in reserving your coaching efforts for financial advisors and teams who meet the following five criteria.

FIVE CRITERIA FOR FINANCIAL ADVISOR OR TEAM COACHING CANDIDATES

1. They must have a strong desire to build or restructure their financial practice to successfully attract, service, and retain the loyalty of affluent investor clients – and be willing to work hard to achieve this transition within the next 18 to 24 months. In most cases, the gap between where they are now and what they're trying to become is substantial. Coaching can help advisors stay focused and forge ahead; but only a strong desire to succeed on the part of the advisors will give them the staying power they need.

2. They must recognize the importance of balancing what they currently do (the day-to-day operations of their business) with what they need to begin doing differently – and be willing to make sure that neither

is neglected. There are a couple issues here. First, they are taking a risk when they establish 5-year business development goals that are a significant stretch from where they are now. So, the "business as usual" part of their day helps to reduce the "risky business" feeling of stepping outside their comfort zone. Second, as financial advisors become more and more successful in their efforts to attract and service affluent clients, they will clearly see that there is little value in many of the activities that seemed so important only a few months ago. That clear vision will make it easier to abandon old habits as they strive to develop new habits that are consistent with the activities relative to operating a successful 21st Century Financial Practice.

3. They must be committed to action and willing to change – and believe that the FastTrack Coaching Process will enable them to accelerate their efforts toward achieving their goals. Their desire to build something must be fueled by action and a willingness to embrace the changes that result.

4. They must enthusiastically participate in the contracting, work commitment, and review meeting format that is an integral part of the FastTrack Coaching Process. This will only happen when they can see the value of repeating the contract/work/review cycle over and over until they achieve their goals.

5. They must be willing to accept the guidance and support of the manager serving as their coach. Lone Rangers, even those with a faithful sidekick, need not apply. As a manager, you know enough to leave some experienced and competent people alone as long as they meet production goals. Those will not be the people seeking a coaching relationship – at least not at first.

Never assume that a given financial advisor or team, meets your criteria. Teams are particularly complicated because of the variety of people involved. Establish your criteria, in your own words, and create a document to be signed by any financial advisor interested in establishing a coaching relationship with you. Review the criteria with every potential coaching candidate, ask for their reaction, and have them sign the document before moving on to the next step.

Keep in mind that even a signed document is no guarantee that you have initiated a FastTrack Coaching relationship. A financial advisor who cleverly disguises avoidance traps as constructive activity can sabotage best intentions and signed documents. Therefore it's important that specific business development activities consistently force the financial advisor being coached, out of his or her respective comfort zone.

Lawrence was a perfect example of what appeared to be an eager financial advisor looking for help in building his business. A veteran financial advisor of seven years, Lawrence was 45 years old and in his third career. His first job out of college was teaching high school math. After a few years, he went back to school and earned a Master's Degree in Engineering, which landed him a job as a project supervisor with a large construction firm. After nearly a decade of dealing with contractors, unions, and production delays, Lawrence decided to follow his cousin's career path and become a financial advisor.

Impressed with Lawrence's education and professionalism, his first manager took a liking to him and teamed him up with a 70-year-old veteran who was preparing to retire. Six years and two managers later, Lawrence had a mature 50 million dollar book and had become chronically plateaued.

Bruce, the new manager fresh out of branch manager training and anxious to coach his financial advisors into the 21st century, conducted a branch meeting, gave a powerful PowerPoint presentation about the benefits of a coaching relationship, and made an offer to personally coach anyone who was serious about growing their business. Lawrence was the first to raise his hand and ask for Bruce's help.

Three months later, Bruce's patience had run thin. When he called my office, he explained his frustrations: "Lawrence will do every project I ask as long as it doesn't require talking to an affluent prospect. He has excellent contacts, makes a great first impression, and is as honest as the day is long; but I can't find a way to get him to do what he needs to do. I think he's afraid to sell."

My advice was simple. "Select one specific business development activity for Lawrence to complete on a daily basis for two weeks. Hold him strictly accountable, and if he hasn't dramatically improved his efforts, officially sever your coaching relationship with him."

In order to be an effective FastTrack coach, you must want to help people. But that can create Lawrence-type situations if you're not careful. Coaching requires time and energy, neither of which you have in abundance. It's important to choose carefully. Yes, the Lawrence's of the industry are often sincere, and some can even be helped. Anyone can be helped if they are willing to help themselves. The secret to not wasting three months on someone is to make certain that you define specific fixed daily activities as a prerequisite for an ongoing coaching relationship.

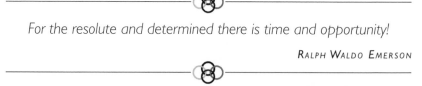

For the resolute and determined there is time and opportunity!

RALPH WALDO EMERSON

Following are some preliminary indicators that can be helpful in making the right choices, as you consider the past and ponder the future.

Looking Back

First, review the previous year with each financial advisor to determine what they achieved, how they did it, and why. This will help clarify how considerable a transition they will have to make. We suggest you ask them to gather the following information so you can review it together.

Even if you already have some of this information, ask them to organize it and bring it to you. It will tell you a lot about how they will respond to a coaching relationship.

1. Their current client profile

- Number of current clients – and how many households that represents.

- Number and profile of new clients added during the past 12 months.

- Number of clients lost to competition (not death) during the past 12 months.

Distribute those current, added, and lost clients in the chart below.

Category	Income	Assets	Current	Added	Lost
Superrich	$10 million or more	$100 million or more			
Rich	$1 million to $10 million	$10 million to $100 million			
Upper-Middle	$75,000 to $1 million	$500,000 to $10 million			
Middle	$35,000 to $75,000	$55,000 to $500,000			
Lower-Middle	$15,000 to $35,000	$10,000 to $55,000			

Adapted from: Forbes, October 11, 1999

2. Their current activity profile

- Production over the past 12 months.

- Production growth (or loss) over the past 12 months.

- Current assets under management.

- New assets acquired over the past 12 months.

- The criteria they currently use to screen and select prospective clients to pursue, not the methods they use to attract them. That will come later.

3. Current investment positions

- Ask them how many different positions they currently manage: individual securities, mutual funds, and third party money managers.

- Discuss how many positions they think they can effectively manage.

- If appropriate, ask how it might improve their business if they reduced the positions they managed by 25 percent (pick your own figure).

4. The current advisory team

- Who they work with on a co-equal basis, if anyone.

- Who assists them, if anyone – and whether it's on a full or part-time basis.

5. The current business development strategy

- Percent of total time spent on business development planning and implementation. This is the safest way to determine how important business development is to them.

- The specific business development methods they use – seminars, direct mail, cold calling, affinity groups, networking, referrals they solicit, etc.

- For each method, ask them to explain how effective or ineffective it has been for them – and why.

- Ask them to summarize their thoughts and impressions about their business development efforts over the past 12 months – the good, bad, and ugly!

6. Current planning efforts

- Do they have a written business plan?

- If so, how often do they review the plan? How closely have they followed this plan over the past 12 months?

7. Current challenges

- Ask them to look back over the past 12 months and identify the three greatest challenges they faced in their business. Have them describe these challenges in writing – ranking them in the order of priority.

- For each challenge, have them describe what they did to meet that challenge and detail the outcome of that effort.

Remember, all the above information should be gathered in written form. As you review the responses, particularly consider the following elements.

- The present number of clients in the Upper-Middle to Superrich categories. This will tell you how large their base is for future networking and referrals.

- The criteria currently used to screen and select prospective clients. This will tell you the stretch they will have to make to raise their minimum investable asset level.

- Determine whether there is any commonality in the positions held by their top 25 clients, and how accurately they follow the positions of the clients representing 80 percent of their business. Do they have a system that enables them to manage positions across all of their accounts? Do they use the firm's resources and research to help manage their positions? If not, what do they use?

- Their current business development strategy, particularly the methods used. Look for the use of affinity groups, networking, and referrals – which will give them a base and some experience using the tactics required to attract the affluent.

- Whether or not they have a written business plan and, if so, how closely have they followed that plan over the past 12 months. This will tell you how inclined they will, or will not, be toward creating a 5-year business plan – the first step in the 21st Century Financial Practice development process.

- How extensively they wrote about their three greatest challenges – especially what they did to meet the challenges and the resulting outcome. Make note of the following: How aware are they of the current challenges that are confronting them? Are the challenges they identified related to targeting the affluent? How good are they at meeting challenges and turning them into opportunities?

Looking Ahead

During the discussion about the *five criteria* and *Looking Back* information they provide, you should be exploring issues that can help you shape a coaching relationship with them.

Ask each coaching candidate to review what they have written for each of the areas under *Looking Back* and then tell you the changes they would like to see in each area 12 months from now, in terms of the following considerations:

- **Client Profile** – the numbers in each category plus the criteria they will use to screen and select prospective clients.

- **Advisory Team** – how many, what specialties, and who (if they have anyone in mind).

- **Business Development Strategy and Activity** – how much of their time will be spent on business development, the methods they will use, and why they feel those methods will be successful.

- **Planning** – whether they feel a written plan is important, the number of years they feel it should cover, and how it should guide their activity.

- **Investing** – whether it makes sense to have a manageable number of positions, if so how they should begin the process of clarifying the number of positions and type of investments.

You will want to ask them what changes, beyond those already mentioned, they would like you to help them achieve, if you were to coach them over the next 12 months. As you review and discuss each point with them, consider what they wrote as well as the *amount of thought and insight* they invested in providing you with this information.

Meanwhile, you will want to have each financial advisor complete the *Benchmarking Your Future* self-assessment tool, so that they and you will have a clear picture of the gaps that exist between where they are now and where they need to be, in order to successfully attract, service, and retain the loyalty of affluent clients. You can access that tool at no charge on our web site: http://www.oechsli.com/free.htm.

Your final decision to work with a financial advisor in a coaching relationship should be based on three things:

- Does the information they have provided suggest that they have a good foundation upon which to build a 21st Century Financial Practice?

- Are they clear about the gaps revealed in the *Benchmarking Your Future* assessment tool; and are they eager to have you help them close those gaps?

- Does their commitment to the five basic criteria, and the thought, insight, and effort they put into completing this profile, indicate that they have the desire, drive, and work habits necessary to take them from where they are now to where they need to go?

As I said at the beginning of Chapter 2, by selecting carefully, you will dis-cover that coaching enables both you and the financial advisors you coach to achieve considerably more in less time. That is why we believe that when done right, coaching is truly the FastTrack to success.

Always keep in mind that your own resolution to succeed is more important than any other one thing.

ABRAHAM LINCOLN

Incidentally, Lawrence's coaching relationship took an interesting path. Within two weeks of calling my office, Bruce severed his coaching rela-tionship with Lawrence. After contemplating yet another career change, Lawrence contacted my office to inquire about entering into a coaching relationship with us, not revealing any of his history regarding his former coaching relationship with Bruce. Without knowing any of this background at the time, we turned him down.

It was apparent to our staff that Lawrence needed to determine whether he was willing to help himself. We recommended that he invest in our *Creating a 21st Century Financial Practice* tool kit, complete the benchmark-ing form; begin to work through the action plan and then meet with his manager. It was only later that we discovered the connection between Bruce and Lawrence

At the time of this writing, Bruce still does not have an official coaching relationship with Lawrence, but he is helping him work through the tool kit. To Lawrence's credit, he has opened three new affluent relationships over a two-month period and has recommitted himself to his career as a financial advisor. My suspicion is that a new and improved coaching rela-tionship between Bruce and Lawrence is on the horizon.

This is a good place to leave you with a word of caution. *Looking Back* can be frightening; it is not very different from someone who is terribly out of shape undergoing a complete medical physical. Attempting to move too fast, probe too deeply, or discuss every area that needs to be addressed will probably overwhelm most financial advisors and could shut down a potentially successful coaching relationship.

Few financial advisors or teams are comfortable with the profile of their current client base. Most recognize the benefits of having more high-quality clients and fewer smaller clients. But this understanding is on an intellectual level and your challenge is to get that understanding to be experiential. As a FastTrack coach, you want your financial advisors and teams who need more affluent clients to do specific activities that will enable them to attract one high quality client at a time.

In the same vein, I can remember a $600,000 producer with 120 million dollars in assets who had over 3,000 positions in her book of business. Wow! You can imagine how overwhelmed this financial advisor was when it came down to doing something to consolidate the number of investment positions in her book. She was completely overwhelmed and about ready to shut down. However, by focusing on consolidating the positions of her top 25 clients, she was able to begin making slow forward progress.

Your job as a FastTrack coach is to help individuals and teams maintain their commitment and momentum. That is precisely why you will discover the FastTrack Action Agreements described in Chapter 5 to be an effective tool for you and for those you are coaching. And in Chapter 4 you learn how to form your own FastTrack Coaching Action Agreements.

CHAPTER 4

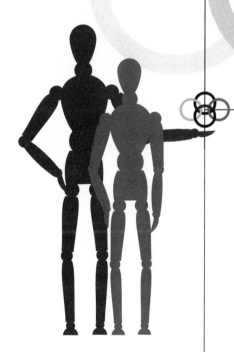

ESTABLISHING FASTTRACK ACTION AGREEMENTS

In life, as in Chess, forethought wins.
CHARLES BUXTON

The most important quality I look for in a player is accountability. You've got to be accountable for who you are. It's too easy to blame things on someone else.
LENNY WILKINS

You are now at the heart of the FastTrack Coaching process. Action Agreements create the contract/work/review cycle that defines the coaching intervention necessary to help individuals and teams move quickly toward their goal.

The FastTrack Action Agreement

Below is an overview of the steps required to form an action agreement with the individual or team you will coach. Following the overview, each step is discussed in greater detail.

The FastTrack Action Agreement

1. Review the related performance gaps (as determined by the Benchmarking Your Future tool) and define the *goal* to be achieved and the *target date for completion.*

2. Identify the *fixed daily activities* necessary to achieve the stated goal and determine the *pattern of achievement* required for each activity.

3. Identify any *performance obstacles* to overcome – reasons the person is *not able* and/or *not willing* to do what is required.

4. Contract for the *support* needed to overcome those obstacles.

5. Schedule a *review meeting* on or immediately after the goal completion target date, when the following will be reviewed:

   • What was achieved.

   • What was not achieved and what corrective action will be taken.

   • What each of you learned that can be applied to the next contract.

One of the first questions you may ask, as you contemplate defining your Action Agreement, is how large a "chunk" should I tackle? That's what we asked ourselves when we were defining the 14 Action Agreements in

Chapter 5. Those suggested Action Agreements can help you define your own agreements, but keep in mind that each individual or team you coach brings a different mix of expertise and experience to the table. Once the right "chunk" is selected, here's what you need to do.

Step 1

Define the goal and determine a completion target date.

1. Define the *goal* to be achieved. The key is to focus on the outcome – what will be in place when the goal is achieved. Use specific and concrete descriptions as much as possible.

2. Determine a *target date for completion*. When the goal to be achieved is clear, the next question is "When will it be completed?" Consider the following:

   • This is not the only item on their daily agenda. They now have a double challenge – continue to "make a living" and at the same time prepare for their future. That balance needs to be discussed, and the resulting *target date* needs to be realistic within that context.

   • The more anxious they feel about doing what is required, the greater their tendency will be to push the target date out as far as they can. Remind them that target dates can be adjusted. Urge them to set a date that will FastTrack them ahead – realistically.

Step 2

Identify Fixed Daily Activities and Patterns of Achievement for each.

In order to achieve their goal, there are important recurring tasks that they must do on a regular basis. Some *Fixed Daily Activities (FDAs)* will be done daily – others weekly, or even monthly. The key is that there are important things they must *do on a daily basis*, even if the specifics differ from day to day.

The *Pattern of Achievement* for each FDA will differ.

- Some FDAs will actually be a series of steps — and you will need to help them define a completion date for each step. It's an FDA because taking a FastTrack approach means working at it daily.

- Other FDAs will be done on a regular schedule — so you will need to help them list those FDAs and record the appropriate Pattern of Achievement in their daily planner.

Step 3

Identify any Performance Obstacles to overcome.

Performance Obstacles are the reasons the person you are coaching is not able and/or not willing to do what is required (to perform FDA's) in order to achieve his or her goal for a given action agreement. The key to success is to recognize obstacles and deal with them immediately.

By the time you reach this point, you will probably know if any obstacles exist. You will also have some ideas about why they exist and the impact they will have.

But don't assume! Point out what you have heard and observed, and ask for their input. Come to agreement about what those obstacles are. Remind them that your next step will be to "contract" the support you will provide them in their efforts to break through and overcome any obstacles that exist.

Common reasons people are not able to perform.

A. They don't know what to do. For example, knowing that they need to complete a 5-year business plan is not enough. They also need to know what elements must be included in that plan.

Chuck's wealth management team was the poster child of process and efficiency. Their 5-year business plan was a 95 page bound document. It read like an MBA thesis or the plan of someone trying to raise venture capital. Everyone who read it showered the team with praise.

My response was slightly different. I asked Chuck how closely they had followed their business plan over the past 18 months. My interest was in practical application. "To be brutally honest, we haven't done a very good job of doing what we needed to do in order to bring in the number and quality of new clients we had committed to in our business plan," confessed Chuck after a difficult pause.

As I probed a bit deeper, it became apparent that all three senior financial advisors were uncomfortable with the idea of proactively prospecting serious money. In less than 10 minutes of discussion, the entire team admitted to falling in love with their planning process, at the expense of doing the necessary activities to attract new affluent clients. Subconsciously, they were all hoping that their reputation and professionalism would be what attracted new high quality business.

Probing even further, I uncovered the real reason they felt so uncomfortable with proactively prospecting. The bottom line with this high-powered group was that they really didn't know what to do. I helped them simplify their business plan into two pages with specific business development activities for each partner to be completed every day. Their manager was then brought into the loop, when previously he had nothing to do with the daily execution of their plan, so they now hold weekly accountability meetings. Four months later, more was going on than had happened during the previous two years. That's because they knew what to do, and were doing it.

B. **They don't know how to do it**. Using our previous example, even if they know which elements to include in their 5-year business plan, they may not know how to pull together the information they need and make the wisest choices about the numbers involved.

Can you imagine a veteran wealth management team not knowing how to conduct a first meeting presentation with an affluent prospect? Don't laugh – it's more common than you might think. Let's face it, many financial advisors developed bad habits in the '90s. Business was much easier in the midst of an unprecedented bull market. Now they are being forced to apply their skills, and many are not certain "how" to do what they know they need to do. Bill and Jennifer are a perfect example.

Bill and Jennifer have been a team for almost 10 years. They initially came together to share seminar expenses, which led to joint seminars and eventually evolved into becoming a team. They were a team before teams were popular. They have been extremely successful, growing their business to three million dollars in production and 500 million dollars in assets. But for a couple of years, growth stalled causing their business to be off 25 percent. This created a delayed coaching opportunity as they, without any assistance, revamped their business plan to focus on attracting 3 to 5 million dollar level prospects.

Unfortunately, neither Bill nor Jennifer knew how to market to this level of affluence – and they were too successful to ask for, or be offered, any advice. After all, in Jennifer's words, "We'd gotten large enough that we no longer had to pay for seminars, so we felt as though we might as well hold them ourselves since they don't cost us any money. After all, they are the marketing vehicle that got us to where we are."

Then Bill spoke up. "The seminars may not have cost us anything, but we did pay a price," he explained. "I'm embarrassed to tell you that we recently blew off a Sunday afternoon cookout at a good client's house, rationalizing that we were tired since we had conducted a seminar on Friday evening and needed time with our families. What made it even worse is that when I called on Monday to apologize for not making it, my client informed me he held the cookout for us – so we could mingle within his centers-of-influence."

At that point they admitted they were reluctant to professionally travel in those circles because they weren't certain how to prospect in that kind of social gathering. This three million dollar level team did not know how to network, ask for introductions, or capitalize on word-of-mouth influence!

When we conducted a skill-training workshop for their entire complex and involved the management team, Bill and Jennifer were called upon to be accountable and use what they were learning. They had the opportunity to practice their newfound skills live by being accountable to their branch manager for doing specific fixed daily activities.

If we did all the things we are capable of doing, we would literally astound ourselves.

THOMAS EDISON

Common reasons people are not willing to perform.

A. **They don't know why it's important to do something.** There is a lot of pressure to target affluent investors today. Your financial advisors may think they are already doing it. Or they may think they are doing well enough and are not sure how all this effort to transform their business will benefit them. Remember that people must discover their own reasons for doing something, especially when so much effort and change is involved. Then again questioning the importance of something could also stem from low self-confidence.

Simply telling Jennifer and Bill to abandon seminars after years of success and to start networking would probably have fallen on deaf ears. They had to learn that seminars would not work when targeting the affluent. Through the unfortunate incident with their client, they discovered the power of networking. Low self-confidence in their networking skills also played a role. Fortunately, they became convinced enough to begin learning and using the skills they needed, as they recognized why those networking activities and skills are so important.

B. **They believe something else is more important.** This could come from personal conviction, or it could come from pressures placed on them by their company and/or their manager. They may have clients for whom they have "a heart," and they may not want to abandon them or the niche they represent. They may want to specialize in a specific financial advisory area rather than build a wealth management team that provides all the categories of services. Or, maybe they are still being pushed to keep adding clients (any clients) using the same old sales and marketing methods.

You can see how this factored into Jennifer and Bill's situation. Although no one tried to place direct pressure on them in a specific direction, reluctance on the part of others to give them advice because of their past success helped convince them to continue showing everyone how successful their approach was. Achieving success through seminars was the "something else" they believed was more important. When the success of their seminars dwindled and the "teachable moment" of the lost opportunity at their client's cookout occurred, they recognized that they needed to take another approach.

Step 4
Contract for the support needed to overcome obstacles.

In this case, *you are that support.* You may need to involve others, but all support will come through you, so that you can monitor the support being provided and observe how the person or team you are coaching utilizes the support.

The specific support you provide must be clearly defined in the following terms.

- *What* you will provide and when you will provide it.

- The expected *influence* it will have on their efforts to achieve their goal.

The support you provide can be in many forms.

- As simple as checking with them every other day to see how they are progressing.

- As concrete as providing important company records.

- As creative as pulling a few people together who are further down the road in achieving a 21st Century Financial Practice and having them explain how they set up their metrics system — reporting on the successes as well as the failures.

In the case of Bill and Jennifer, the contract for support initially involved a skills workshop for the entire complex. Training all financial advisors was a strategic coaching move to protect the ego of a three million dollar team while making certain that they received the necessary support.

Often the contract for support is as simple as getting permission to hold whoever is being coached accountable on a daily basis and suggesting that you will be dropping by periodically, possibly even daily, to check on their progress. This was what Chuck's team and their manager agreed upon; and following their skill training, Bill and Jennifer formed a similar agreement with their manager; one that focused specifically on accountability for doing their fixed daily activities.

Support always works best when the people you are coaching tell you they need it, rather than you telling them they need it.

Step 5

Schedule a Review Meeting.

Here are three points to remember when scheduling a Review Meeting.

- The best time to schedule the Review Meeting is at the target date.

- Keep the originally scheduled Review Meeting date even if, or especially if, it becomes clear that the Target Date is not going to be met.

- If the Review Meeting is held before the goal has been achieved, schedule another Review Meeting on or right after the *new* Target Date you establish. Continue this as often as necessary until the goal has been achieved. This will remind them to be as realistic as possible when setting Target Dates.

At each Review Meeting, identify and review the following three things.

- What *was achieved?* Draw out their "good feelings" about the achievement.

- What *was not achieved?* Determine what it will take to complete the contract and get started right away. Note on the current Action Agreement Form that the goal remains incomplete.

- What have each of you *learned from this experience* that can be applied to the next Action Agreement?

Celebrate the achievements – and begin working on the next FastTrack Action Agreement!

Using Checkpoints

Checkpoints simply involve "dropping in" on the individual or team you are coaching; to check on their performance, but primarily to see how they are getting along. Your focus should be on answering any questions and encouraging them.

In Chapter 1, we noted that one of the three critical managerial support factors that impacts a financial advisor's loyalty to his or her firm is receiving the manager's help with maintaining a good level of personal health. This need for a supported sense of well-being is particularly strong.

As you review the Action Agreements in Chapter 5, you will find a list of "Potential blockages you may encounter" at the end of each one. When you are dropping in for your checkpoints, look for signs of these blockages and always be prepared with encouragement and possible solutions.

Following are some pointers to consider when scheduling your checkpoints.

- As you form each Action Agreement, make special note of any blockages you encountered during the discussion, especially any expressed anxiety about their willingness or ability to achieve the goal. Those are the things you want to be alert to during checkpoints.

- Schedule *checkpoints* in your daily planner. Always plan to go to them rather than calling them in to meet with you.

- When you make your *checkpoint* visits, keep them upbeat but focused. Don't simply ask how they're doing – ask how they're doing with a specific activity (a specific fixed daily activity or a potential blockage you noted earlier). Make suggestions and offer help, if needed. Let them know that you are there for them and always leave behind a word of encouragement.

I can live for two months on a good compliment.

MARK TWAIN

QUARTERLY REVIEW

Establish that Quarterly Reviews will be held, and then schedule your first one at the same time you are working with them on your first FastTrack Action Agreement. About two weeks before the first Quarterly Review meeting, send them a reminder asking them to be prepared to report on their progress to date. Ask them to highlight what they have accomplished, what went well, what didn't go well, why, and what they did about it.

Consider the following when preparing your agenda for the Quarterly Review meeting.

- Have some type of brief celebration (lunch, movie tickets, drinks after work) after the progress report has been given.

- Review what remains to be accomplished – you can use the remaining FastTrack Action Agreements as the basis for that discussion.

- Ask the individual or team what they have learned that they feel will enable them to perform better during the next quarter.

- Ask them what potential obstacles they envision and discuss how they can be prevented.

- Give them an honest appraisal of their progress, followed with words of encouragement for the tasks ahead.

- Get a clear commitment for the specific actions to be taken that are outside the Action Agreements and their accompanying fixed daily activities, projects, or skill training.

- Schedule your next Quarterly Review meeting.

As you can see, coaching is not a constant "looking over their shoulder" type of management process. Once you have a given Action Agreement linked to a scheduled Quarterly Review, you step in (or intervene) only when you agreed to when you created the agreement – or when things become bogged down. The Quarterly Review is important because of the extended period of time it takes to complete all 14 Action Agreements. Checkpoints are to be used more for encouragement. When you take the time and effort to work out good Action Agreements, the individuals and teams you coach will know exactly what they need to do and what help they can expect from you.

Remember that coaching is extremely personal. No two financial advisors or teams are alike, regardless of outward appearances. Adapting your

Action Agreements to fit the individuals being coached is the secret to ongoing coaching success.

*This is not easy, this effort, day after day, week after week,
to keep up, but it is essential.*

Vince Lombardi

Your FastTrack Coaching objective is to make certain that the people you are coaching are fully engaged in their individual *Achievement Cycles*. You will learn more about this cycle and how to use it as a common thread for all of your coaching in Chapter 8. For now, keep in mind that people achieve by doing specific activities linked to a measurable goal, regardless of what they might be thinking or how they feel. Your coaching will help them to keep that focus clear.

CHAPTER 5

FASTTRACK AGREEMENTS FOR BUILDING A 21ST CENTURY FINANCIAL PRACTICE

Nothing is particularly hard if you divide it into small jobs.

RAY KROC

Obstacles don't have to stop you. If you run into a wall, don't turn around and give up. Figure out how to climb it, go through it, or work around it.

MICHAEL JORDAN

FastTrack suggests speed. Granted, there is a bit of duplicity in this. In one breath I'm talking about speed; in the next I'm telling you it takes about 18 months for those you coach to completely reposition, rebuild, and rebrand their business into a 21st Century Financial Practice.

As you look for a way to help the people you coach to optimize the time required to build a 21st Century Financial Practice you need a process; a tool that will keep those you are coaching from becoming overwhelmed while they simultaneously strengthen their commitment to do what they have agreed to do. The tool we have developed for that purpose is the Action Agreement described in Chapter 4.

Even more important than any specific Action Agreement, is the role these agreements play for you and for those you are coaching. The idea is to coach people into taking one or two strategic steps at a time, hold them accountable for doing whatever is required, and then build the next step on the heels of the previous one.

This chapter breaks down the overall process into 14 suggested FastTrack Action Agreements. The emphasis is on:

- **Chunking** – breaking down the coaching process into manageable "chunks," realizing that you may find reasons to adjust those boundaries with a particular individual or team.

- **Sequencing** – completing the first two Agreements before anything else, and then selecting the appropriate sequence based on the expertise, experience, and desire of the individual or team you are coaching.

- **Anticipating** – identifying potential blockages that may arise in each of the "chunks."

- **Doing** – continuing the emphasis on "doing" as the first step of The Achievement Cycle (see Chapter 8), the one thing over which the people you are coaching have complete control.

How the FastTrack Action Agreements are Organized

Each suggested Action Agreement contains the following three elements:

1. A **focus** (choose from the following)

   - Building Their Business

   - Providing Financial Advisory Services

   - Establishing Operational Efficiency

   - Building Client Loyalty

2. A **goal** and **target date**

   - An explanation of the results that need to be achieved, based primarily on the *Benchmarking Your Future* performance gaps relative to the goal.

   - Suggestions on how to approach the tasks.

   - Determine the target date.

3. **Potential blockages you may encounter** – What the Psychology of Performance tells us about the destructive thinking, habits, goal motivation, and achievement cycle issues that might exist with this specific goal.

   Each blockage, as it occurs, actually represents an opportunity to Fast-Track the process ahead. Explain that you appreciate how they are feeling, but until they actually **do** what is required, they will not fully recognize the importance and value of what they are being asked to do.

As you create the Action Agreement with them – keep them focused on doing what they agreed to do. You will also want to include any support to be provided that has been agreed upon and schedule your review meeting.

Sequencing the FastTrack Action Agreements

These Action Agreements are designed to FastTrack the individuals and teams you coach through the four 21st Century Financial Practice development processes – Building Their Business, Providing Financial Advisory Services, Establishing Operational Efficiency, and Building Client Loyalty. Although the agreements are numbered from 1 to 14, it is not necessary to sequence them in that order.

A **sequencing strategy** will unfold as you initiate the FastTrack Coaching relationship (Chapter 3) with the individual or team, and as you assess their level of expertise and experience in each of the four processes. We suggest that you approach the sequencing decision with the following factors in mind.

1. Have them complete Agreements 1 and 2 first in every case. That establishes their 5-Year Business Plan and Metrics Scorecard System as the foundation for everything else. The business plan is what pulls them ahead and the scorecard system measures their progress.

2. Recognize that there is a building block sequence of agreements within each process.

   - Building Their Business – Agreements 3, 4, and 5.

   - Providing Financial Advisory Services – Agreements 6, 7, and 8.

   - Establishing Operational Efficiency – Agreements 9, 10, 11, and 12.

   - Building Client Loyalty – Agreements 13 and 14.

3. When building a team based 21st Century Financial Practice, the agreements under the Providing Financial Advisory Services and Establishing Operational Efficiency processes need to be started early, possibly in parallel with each other – and certainly before you begin Agreements 3, 4, and 5 under Building Their Business. A review of these 14 Fast-

Track Action Agreements will help to clarify the importance of taking this into consideration when developing your sequencing strategy.

We won championships at Duke
because of what happened behind closed doors.

CHRISTIAN LAETTNER (DUKE 1988-92)

FASTTRACK ACTION AGREEMENT 1

Focus: Building Their Business

Goal and target date: The goal is to complete a **5-Year Business Plan.** You may already require them to complete a business plan. However, this plan covers a five year period and is directly related to building a 21st Century Financial Practice. They need to address client profile, advisory team, business strategy, and quality of life issues. It should take them no longer than two or three days to achieve this goal. They may need to check out a few things and talk to a few people to make the required decisions, but those tasks should not be dragged out. This is where the FastTrack concept can become firmly established.

Potential blockages you may encounter:

- Not sold on planning – not confident with the planning process.

- Difficulty making decisions about their desired future state.

- Being proud of what they have already achieved and not being convinced they should go in a new direction at this time.

FASTTRACK ACTION AGREEMENT 2

Focus: Building Their Business

Goal and target date: The goal is to create a **Metrics Scorecard System** that will keep them focused on strategies and tactics that go beyond production numbers and include activities that indicate future success. We suggest developing a set of weekly, quarterly, and yearly (years 1 through 5) scorecards plus a list of **Fixed Daily Activities (FDAs)** needed to implement and measure those indicators. After developing the scorecards the emphasis shifts to doing those Fixed Daily Activities (FDAs) they have identified as they work toward completing their first Weekly Scorecard. Encourage them to spend no more than a week to complete this Action Agreement.

Potential blockages you may encounter:

- Still not sold on planning – not comfortable with the scorecard monitoring process.

- Difficulty making decisions about what future measurements should be.

- Struggling with accountability.

FastTrack Action Agreement 3

Focus: Building Their Business

Goal and target date: The goal is to create the **Ideal Client Profile** they really believe in – after carefully analyzing their current client base, exploring the opportunities within affluent market segments, and completing a study to see where they concentrate their time and activity. They should be able to draft an Ideal Client Profile within a week, but they also need to spend at least two weeks conducting a Time and Activity study to determine where they currently focus their efforts.

Potential blockages you may encounter:

- Discovering that they do not know many of their clients well enough to analyze them.

- Acknowledging that they probably have too many clients, most of whom will fall below the minimum investable asset level they are being challenged to establish.

- Believing that they don't know many affluent prospects or where to find them.

- Feeling that the *Weekly Time and Activity Log* is simply busy work, and not worth the effort.

- Reluctance to define an *Ideal Client Profile* that "raises the bar" and places many of their current clients below the minimum investable asset level they have established.

FastTrack Action Agreement 4

Focus: Building Their Business

Goal and Target Date: The goal is to begin **networking** to attract affluent prospects who match their *Ideal Client Profile*. They will also produce a highly professional looking **promotional piece** that clearly communicates their value commitment, their Financial Advisory Process, and the benefits of working with them. This should be ready for the printer within two or three weeks.

Potential blockages you may encounter:

- Wanting a slick piece that's all about them (and their ego) rather than focusing on the benefits to the client through the Financial Advisory Process by which they deliver value.

- Not understanding why the promotional piece should not be mailed, and should only be used to explain their value commitment, Financial Advisory Process and benefits, in a one-on-one interaction with the prospective client. Then, and only then, should the piece be left with the prospect.

FastTrack Action Agreement 5

Focus: Building Their Business

Goal and Target Date: The goal is to begin **qualifying and closing** the affluent prospects they are now attracting. This contract begins at a designated time, but there is no end to the activities associated with attracting, qualifying, and closing new affluent clients who match their new *Ideal Client Profile*.

Potential blockages you may encounter:

- Difficulty making the transition from doing busy work and making phone calls in the quiet of their office to interacting with people outside the office. Implementing these Tactical How-To's requires getting up and going out. Some will be eager to get started; others will be stretched beyond their comfort zone.

- Not accepting that the networking-related tactics are more effective than the tactics they have been using – such as cold calling, seminars, and mailings, with very few referrals.

- Hanging on to the old Wall Street sales and marketing tactic habits, rather than replacing them with new habits centered around networking, obtaining introductions and referrals; and going to where affluent prospects hang out, listening for openings to present their value proposition, asking for appointments – and then qualifying and closing prospects.

*A leader cannot just tell people what to do
and then expect them to perform.*

MIKE KRZYZEWSKI "COACH K"

FASTTRACK ACTION AGREEMENT 6

Focus: Providing Financial Advisory Services

Goal and Target Date: The goal is to establish a **Development Plan** that will prepare them to provide solutions in each of the eight financial advisory categories suggested. It should include one to three categories that they personally plan to focus on, any certification they intend to pursue, and how they plan to add to their wealth management team in order to provide expertise in the remaining categories. The challenge will be to identify qualified people to provide competent service in the other categories – and determine whether to hire them or arrange a strategic alliance with them. That could take three weeks to accomplish, but they probably can begin another Action Agreement during that time.

Potential blockages you may encounter:

- Feeling overwhelmed with the thought of providing competent solutions in all eight financial advisory categories.

- Difficulty making a decision about working toward any certification.

- Uncertainty about where to specialize, who to add to their team, and where to find outside experts for potential strategic alliances.

FastTrack Action Agreement 7

Focus: Providing Financial Advisory Services

Goal and Target Date: The goal is to design a client-focused, client-driven **Financial Advisory Process** and prepare to competently **interview and profile affluent clients.** This Financial Advisory Process should be designed with care. They may want to see what others are doing and they certainly will want to talk with other team members. Base the Target Date on the amount of research and collaboration that will be required – probably one to three weeks.

Potential blockages you may encounter:

- Difficulty making the mental and behavioral shift from administering *transactions* to implementing a long-term, on-going financial advisory process.

- Talking too much, rather than listening, when using an interview process to profile affluent clients.

- Not knowing how to use the profile information to personalize the Financial Advisory Process.

FastTrack Action Agreement 8

Focus: Providing Financial Advisory Services

Goal and Target Date: The goal is to develop a **Financial Organizer** binder with dividers – to be given to each client to store the documentation relating to the development and implementation of the financial solutions that emerge during the Financial Advisory Process. Once their Financial Advisory Process is in place, this should be achieved with only a few hours of effort.

Potential blockages you may encounter:

- Not recognizing how important the Organizer is to the successful ongoing management of their Financial Advisory Process.

- Not being able to create a functional Organizer – one that contains all financial documents and accomplishes two objectives: (1) Organizes the documents for quick reference by the client and (2) Helps facilitate future Financial Advisory Process related contacts.

FastTrack Action Agreement 9

Focus: Establishing Operational Efficiency

Goal and Target Date: The goal is to **define and initiate team operational efficiency** relating to *areas of responsibility, performance standards, eliminating time wasters*, and *improving team meetings*. Although efforts in these areas need to be ongoing, there are important exercises the team must go through to initiate each one. This should be a cooperative and concentrated effort that takes about a week to initiate – with continued monitoring thereafter.

Potential blockages you may encounter:

- Not believing that these "defining" tasks are necessary for team operational efficiency.

- Continuing habits centered on working independently and difficulty replacing them with habits focused on working collaboratively.

- Not being open and honest about things like time wasters.

FastTrack Action Agreement 10

Focus: Establishing Operational Efficiency

Goal and Target Date: The goal is to **delegate all tasks** and **assign lead role responsibilities** in all areas. We suggest using a series of team meetings with a target completion date one week out. That's only the beginning. These areas of responsibility will need to be monitored and adjustments made as needed.

Potential blockages you many encounter:

- Difficulty making this a team effort. Not wanting to get rid of habits centered around working independently or replace them with habits focused on working collaboratively.

- Not believing that these "defining" tasks are necessary for team operational efficiency.

FastTrack Action Agreement 11

Focus: Establishing Operational Efficiency

Goal and Target Date: The goal is to have each team member working to establish and then achieve **personal development goals**. The target date should focus on a deadline for each team member to have his or her Development Goals list completed. One week should be sufficient.

Potential blockages you may encounter:

- Lack of confidence in their ability to achieve a new goal.

- Not recognizing the benefits that personal development will produce, personally and for the team.

FastTrack Action Agreement 12

Focus: Establishing Operational Efficiency

Goal and Target Date: The goal is to have a valued, user-friendly **Team Documentation Manual** completed and available for daily use. This should be done right after the personal development goals are completed – and it should take about a week to create.

Potential blockages you might encounter:

- Not accepting the importance of documentation – and not using the *Documentation Manual* to actually guide team operations and orient new team members.

FastTrack Action Agreement 13

Focus: Building Client Loyalty

Goal and Target Date: The goal is to implement specific **strategies for building client loyalty** and, in the process, make client loyalty the responsibility of each and every team member, each and every day. Selecting and implementing the strategies that will have both immediate and ongoing impact should take the team about 30 days.

Potential blockages you may encounter:

- Not believing that they can or should expend so much effort in knowing each client.

- Not willingly admitting mistakes or seeing that identifying them is vital to improvement.

- Thinking that any formal effort to log new ideas is unnecessary.

- Resisting specific strategies for building client loyalty – those that involve inconvenience on their part.

FastTrack Action Agreement 14

Focus: Building Client Loyalty

Goal and Target Date: The goal is to have a **Client Loyalty Profile** completed for each key client, strategies in place for improving client loyalty, and a schedule for updating the profiles every six months. Assigning specific clients to specific team members and then coming together to review each profile should take about two weeks.

Potential blockages you may encounter:

- Resistance to expending time and effort to create a Profile for every key client.

- Rushing to get the building of the 21st Century Financial Practice effort over and done with.

Good ideas can come from anywhere and everywhere.

Mike Krzyzewski "Coach K"

Each one of these action agreements is merely a means to an end, so be careful not to get bogged down in the process of coaching. This can easily happen and the results will suffer.

Rob, an enlightened manager of a 20 million dollar branch, was sold on the process of coaching. He took it upon himself to select five financial advisors he believed would be worth his time and effort. .

Everyone had pre-work to complete. Rob agreed to personally analyze every aspect of their work. Each financial advisor had business tools developed by the firm and agreed to go through them in their entirety. Because everyone was excited about the concept of performance coaching, Rob thought all was well.

Unfortunately, he had miscalculated. Soon the financial advisors began to grumble about their pre-work. "It takes too much time," was the feedback. "Not all of this is relevant to my business. There's too much redundancy."

But Rob weathered these objections and convinced his financial advisors to stay the course and complete the pre-work. At the same time he found himself spending up to five hours on each financial advisor, a whopping total of 25 hours just to launch the coaching process!

After two coaching meetings, Rob decided to change his tactics. Rather than hold these financial advisors accountable for doing pre-work that could be argued as "questionable," he began to personalize each coaching relationship into a series of FastTrack agreements that linked fixed daily activities directly to building a 21st Century Financial Practice that could successfully attract affluent clients. He stopped simply coaching busy work and began causing results.

Time, energy, and enthusiasm are often wasted when you fall in love with a process at the expense of results. It slowed down the growth of Chuck's wealth management team and it nearly derailed Rob's coaching efforts. It is definitely one of the mistakes you will want to avoid.

Knowing that many of you will take these 14 Action Agreements very literally, I feel compelled to remind you that they are merely tools, designed to guide and enhance your coaching efforts. Don't think that you have to use all 14 Agreements. As your coaching progresses, some agreements that at one time seemed crucial may no longer be relevant. Performance gaps can close in mysterious ways when people become proactive about their growth and development.

I have found Action Agreements 1 and 2 to be a standard, and I strongly recommend that you begin with them. However, there may be occasions when you're working with an advanced team that has already completed the work of those agreements. In such instances, use your common sense and adjust accordingly. A good tactic is to initiate a discussion about the business plan, find out who is doing what, and determine what results have been achieved. Look for specific answers. When a direct question produces a vague response, you have probably uncovered a viable coaching opportunity. That is precisely what happened in Sheila's case.

Sheila's team had a well-written business plan that they proudly displayed in a small 3-ring binder. It was complete with mission statement, production targets, assets targets, new assets projections, fee targets, and specifically delegated areas of responsibility for each team member.

Because of a poor market, a death in the family of a team member, and other external factors, there had been very little accountability for doing what was necessary to transition more business to fees and to bring in new affluent clients. The team rationalized that they were working as hard as ever – answering calls from clients who had lost money and covering for the financial advisor who had to take a lot of personal time in order to attend to family matters. Unfortunately, neither Sheila nor her manager investigated further, so what they had was a good-looking document awaiting execution.

After listening to their story, I realized that my role was to compliment them on their plan and then spank them for their lack of activity in executing! They immediately realized that I wasn't buying into any excuses. They knew that they could have done better, so I simply had them review their plan and develop an Action Agreement that initiated steps to transition clients to fees and develop new relationships in order to attract new money.

As part of our Action Agreement, Sheila and her junior partner committed to do specific fixed daily activities that would make their business plan real.

I share this particular case with you because Sheila's manager was initially so impressed by the team's existing business plan, he assumed that they didn't need to talk about the first two Action Agreements. In his mind, the team just needed to get to work. But in reality they needed to attach commitment, specificity and accountability to their noble document and then get to work.

Although a FastTrack coach needs to be empathetic regarding the events that occur in the lives of the people being coached, excuses must not be accepted over a prolonged period of time. Action agreements are the best solution because the goal to be achieved and the steps required to achieve it are well defined. In the next section we will discuss how the mind works and how it helps to define your coaching activities.

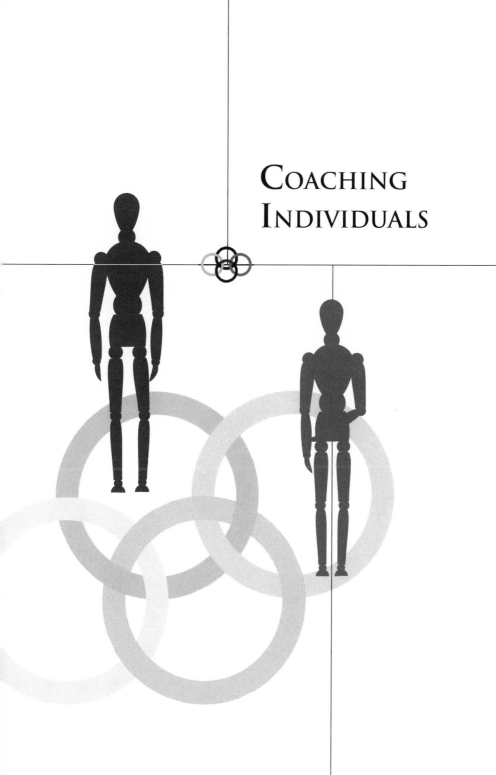

COACHING
INDIVIDUALS

CHAPTER 6

CONSTRUCTIVE MIND POWER AND THE FORCE OF HABIT

We are what we repeatedly do. Excellence then, is not an act, but a habit.

UNKNOWN

It's what you learn after you know it all that counts.

JOHN WOODEN

Years ago, PBS ran two outstanding television series titled *The Mind* and *The Brain*. The fascinating series on the brain was based on science, with Dr. Roger Sperry's split-brain research serving as the headliner. It was extremely informative and answered many questions for the layperson. As a physical human organ, medical and science communities have been able to study the brain in the laboratory quite extensively.

The series on the mind was equally fascinating, but decidedly different. Although the mind has engaged human curiosity since the beginning of time, there are still more questions than answers. Yet, we know much more today than we did 50 years ago about that nebulous area of the mind where neuroscience, psychology, and theology meet. Experts do agree on one thing though, the mind is what sets us apart from every other species on our planet. We have learned that how we think can help us remain in good health or make us prone to continual illness; how we use our mind determines whether we are at peace with ourselves or go through life a nervous wreck.

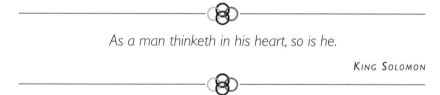

As a man thinketh in his heart, so is he.

KING SOLOMON

It is critical for a FastTrack coach to recognize the power contained within the human mind, because how financial advisors use their minds will determine whether or not they reach their potential and achieve their goals. High achievers have developed the habit of using their minds constructively, a process I refer to as developing *constructive mind power*. Achievers tend to possess good energy, think big, focus on solutions rather than obstacles, attract good things into their lives, and have very little tolerance for their negative mind power counterparts. Napoleon once asked when being briefed about the skills of an excellent young officer, "Is he lucky?" Luck probably had little to do with his success.

Alas, many people, when left to their own resources, focus on problems. They worry too much and focus on what could or did go wrong. This is the result of being conditioned to think this way by parents, teachers, and society in general. Even the news is negative. Teachers tell students how many questions they got wrong and what they do not know. Many parents are also prone to focus attention on what they do not like about their children's behavior or grades, rather than on what they admire. In fact, we are infected with more negative mind power than we realize or care to admit.

So, why is this important information for the FastTrack coach to possess?

Consider this…

- Most people do not *think* big enough.

- An important aspect of building team unity is to recognize individual uniqueness.

- Most people desperately *want* to achieve at a higher level, individually and as a team member.

- Non-performance is frequently mistaken for laziness when it actually stems from self-limiting *habits*.

- Achievement *patterns* are instinctive.

- Adults have a tendency to gravitate to what's *comfortable* (their comfort zone).

- Most people need *help* (coaching) to break out of their comfort zone in order to achieve at a higher level.

- Although it is frequently used as a short-term motivator, *fear* actually holds people back from maximizing their potential.

- Most people only tap into 20 percent or less of their *potential*.

This chapter is the first of three on coaching individuals. Throughout this section, all of the above facts will be clarified and incorporated into your coaching strategy. We begin with constructive mind power and habits.

In a sense, having a working knowledge of the chapters in this section will serve as high-octane fuel for all of your future coaching success. Not many coaches have earned a Ph.D. in Psychology; yet every good coach, whether on the athletic field or in the office, needs to understand the basics of human behavior. It's important to discover how the mind works, what is required to engage people into doing the right activities, how to get people to venture outside of and expand their comfort zone, and what it takes to get people to believe in themselves and think big using constructive mind power. A good coach knows how to use the street-smart psychology learned through the hard-knocks of life, to push the right buttons on an individual basis in order to propel the people he or she coaches toward their potential.

Chance favors the prepared mind.

LOUIS PASTEUR

Rather than bog you down with theoretical debates and vague details about the mind, I believe it will be more effective to lay out a standard and simple overview. My intention is to help you use this powerful tool to better equip every aspect of your coaching efforts.

THE MIND – AN OVERVIEW

One mind, but *two distinctive qualities*:

- **Conscious mind** – our perception of reality. Using all five senses, the conscious mind investigates and interprets all we encounter.

- **Subconscious mind** – records and stores conscious mind input. It does not interpret or evaluate, but simply stores for the long-term, ready to be pulled out and used when needed.

Key Principle: *Whatever you sow into your subconscious mind, you will reap in your daily life.*

One mind, but *functioning in two distinct ways*:

- **Destructively** – focusing on problems; always complaining and blaming. Lacking goal focus, running on negative energy, easily becoming angry.

- **Constructively** – focusing on goals and solutions. Being proactive, helpful, and responsible. Running on "can-do" high energy.

The conscious and subconscious mind each play important roles in shaping our sense of self-worth as we develop confidence in approaching new tasks. We will explore their importance and the impact they have on performance.

THE CONSCIOUS MIND

This is where new information enters the thought process. Using all five senses, the conscious mind investigates and interprets all that it encounters and defines a person's perception of reality.

The conscious mind is very limited, however. Generally, a person can only remember five to seven bits of information at a time, unless he or she has learned to use association techniques that improve memory and make it easier to recall names and other facts. Which explains why after we listen to a lecture, we find that we have to go back and review our notes to dig out all the stuff we missed. That is because the conscious mind can only process one item at a time. And yet, conscious thinking is very important. It's what enables us to concentrate and develop our perception of reality.

Considering the limited amount we can remember and process, we would have serious problems trying to function with only the short-term memory of the conscious mind. Fortunately, that's not the case.

The Subconscious Mind

This is where all the stuff the conscious mind receives and then processes goes. According to the experts, more information is stored in the subconscious mind than exists in all the libraries of the world combined. In fact, everything a person has experienced and felt is stored there. The subconscious mind does not interpret or evaluate as the conscious mind does; it simply stores for the long-term, ready to be pulled to the surface when needed.

Consequently, an important principle emerges from all this.

As you sow in your subconscious mind, so shall you reap in your daily life.

Sowing negative thoughts will reap low self-esteem, resulting in negative attitudes and self-defeating behavior. Sowing positive thoughts will reap healthy self-esteem, resulting in hope, anticipation, and behavior patterns that lead to high performance.

If the conscious mind receives and processes information and perceptions from negative experiences, the resulting negative thinking is transferred to the subconscious mind. Any imbalance on the negative side has a significant impact on a person's sense of self-worth and confidence when faced with a significant performance gap. The reverse is also true.

It is a good idea to begin your interaction with individuals or teams that you are going to coach with the completion of the *Benchmarking Your Future* assessment tool. Typically, they will find a significant number of performance gaps. As they consider beginning an 18 to 24 month process to close those gaps, you will hear constructive and destructive statements.

- **Constructive** statements – expressing a strong desire to close those gaps and showing confidence that they will be successful.

- **Destructive** statements – expressing self-doubt and showing a lack of confidence in their ability to be successful.

The chart below lists some typical constructive and destructive statements that you might hear when individuals are looking at specific performance gaps identified in the *Benchmarking Your Future* tool. As you read each statement, go to the opposite column and read the typical statement you might hear from someone who responds in the opposite way.

CONSTRUCTIVE STATEMENTS	DESTRUCTIVE STATEMENTS
Creating a long-range plan makes sense. I'm looking forward to doing it.	How can I create a long-range plan? I don't know what the industry, or the economy, or potential clients will be like five years from now!
I know I can't become an expert in all eight categories, but I can partner with others. I'll select the two or three that I want to master and begin looking for people who have the additional expertise I need.	Just how much new expertise do I have to develop? Expecting me to learn all about eight financial categories is unreasonable.
I'm ready to abandon my prospecting methods. They don't work anyway. I can't wait to learn new ones that do!	I don't need to learn new methods. The present ones should work OK.
If you'll tell me where I can find information about affluent market segments, I'll start researching them right away.	How am I going to gather information about affluent market segments? I have no idea what they are.

Human beings are the only species on the planet capable of rationalizing their behavior. Yet, according to one of the leading experts on rational decision-making Robyn M. Dawes of Carnegie Mellon University, people do not make rational decisions. In Dawes' words, people are reluctant to 'invalidate' the past. They honor what they have already invested, good or bad.

Consequently, whether it's a brochure that has cost them a lot of money but is now somewhat dated; or an investment process that they learned well but is no longer effective; or a seminar campaign that no longer brings the desired results; or an assistant who is not really up to speed; financial advisors will tend to resist change – even in the midst of compelling logic to do otherwise. Why? – Because we humans rarely stop and think through our decisions logically. Of course later, we are then forced to use thinly veiled destructive statements to defend those choices.

Sally was a high achieving financial advisor. Building a terrific business on cold calling with municipal bonds, she had developed a large asset base over her 23-year career. Recently, she began to lose some key clients and decided that she should again expand her business.

"I just don't buy in to all this fee-based stuff," she explained to me. "I just got a referral who said he was sick and tired of paying a fee for poor performance."

This negative statement was a smoke screen. Sally was actually petrified about changing any aspect of her business. All she knew was the fixed income side of financial services. A decision to build a 21st Century Financial Practice that services the multidimensional financial needs of the affluent would 'invalidate' her past. Consequently, she would welcome and remember any negative statement that would reinforce her decision to remain where she was. In other words, she rationalized her resistance with destructive statements disguised as thoughtful opinions.

EXERCISE 1

Now that you're familiar with the type of constructive and destructive statements you might hear, conduct the following exercise in the two different situations shown.

1. Pre-coaching relationship homework.

A. In Chapter 3, I suggested that you have each financial advisor do some homework prior to entering into a coaching relationship with you. This requires that you to ask them to compile very specific pieces of information about their current business.

B. As you discuss these issues and ask additional questions, pay careful attention to the responses. Note whether they are constructive or destructive.

2. Processing the benchmarking tool.

A. Have an individual or team you expect to coach complete the *Benchmarking Your Future* assessment tool.

B. As you discuss the completed tool with them, ask them to show you the performance gaps they have identified and explain to you what they would like to do about those gaps.

C. As they respond, write down any constructive or destructive statements you hear.

As you review your notes later, what do their comments tell you about their *ability* and their *willingness* to transition to the 21ˢᵗ Century Financial Practice Model?

Your discussion with them will probably give you very little insight into *ability*. But what you will hear a lot about is their *attitude*. If positive, you will hear expressions of excitement and confidence about entering into a coaching situation and about closing those performance gaps. If negative – you'll hear many reasons why coaching is not for them, and why the assessment isn't very good or this just isn't the right approach for them.

Unwillingness easily finds an excuse.

BENJAMIN FRANKLIN

These thought patterns that we have been discussing also transfer into habits that shape a person's comfort zone. Yes, human beings are creatures of habit. We go to bed around the same time every night, attend to our personal hygiene in the same manner every day, sit in the same chair to read or watch television, and even tend to think the same way about the various events that impact our lives. Although we humans are not the only species that develops habits, we are the only species that can make a conscious decision to either break a bad habit or develop a good one. We are creatures of habit, and your challenge as a FastTrack coach is to help break the habits that are holding an individual back and replace them with habits that are constructive.

Habits – An Overview

We are all creatures of *habit*.

- Experts tell us that 80 percent of our behavior is "habit driven."

- *Mental habits* that are stored in our subconscious mind shape and drive our *attitudes*.

- *Doing habits* that are stored in our subconscious mind shape and drive our actions, result in repeatable *behavioral patterns*.

We all operate within a *comfort zone* that is defined by the *mental* and *doing* habits stored in our subconscious mind.

- Our *comfort zone* forms our *self-image* and strongly influences how we perform in all areas of our personal and professional lives.

- *Breaking out* of our *comfort zone* and developing new *attitudes* and *behavioral patterns* are the keys to mastering the inner challenges of high achievement and life itself!

In an amazingly short period of time, how we think and what we do become habits. There are two types that we will consider.

Attitudes. William James, the famous Harvard psychologist, referred to attitudes as "habits of the mind." Attitudes stem from the thoughts stored in our subconscious mind, and they are expressed in the constructive and destructive statements we make.

Behavioral Patterns. We do as we think, and in time those patterns of behavior become habitual.

Even when our attitudes and behavioral patterns tend toward the negative, we learn in time to be comfortable with them. They define our *comfort zone*, which in turn shapes our self-image and strongly influences how we perform in all areas of our personal and professional life.

*Habit is a cable; we weave a thread of it every day
and at last we cannot break it.*

HORACE MANN

By noting the specific attitudes and behavior of the people you are going to coach, you can gain important insight into the boundaries of their comfort zones. Specifically, listen and look for the following clues.

ATTITUDES	BEHAVIOR
Their comments about **setting goals.**	The **specific goals** they set (if any) and their efforts to achieve those goals.
What they say about **gaining new knowledge** and **developing new skills.**	Their **on-going efforts** to **gain new knowledge** and **develop new skills.**
What they tell you about **wanting advice** from you and others.	Their efforts to **seek advice** and how they **receive it.**
Their comments about **accepting change.**	How they respond when **asked to change.**

Exercise 2

To gain further insight into habits, meet with two people you expect to coach. Introduce each of the four topics below, and ask them to tell you their feelings (attitudes) about each.

- Setting and achieving goals.

- Learning new knowledge and skills.

- Accepting advice from others.

- Change.

Take notes as they comment. Typical responses tend to be somewhat defensive and matter-of-fact. When discussing goals, you might hear something like, "I always set goals." As for learning, few will admit they resist. A response like "I'm always open to learning something new" is not unusual. Accepting advice from others can get a bit more personal, so brace yourself for something like, "It depends on the source." The irony regarding change is that most people resist it. But when you ask about it in the context of coaching, you can expect a favorable response such as, "I'll change whatever I'm convinced needs changing."

Continue to ask questions and as they respond, follow-up with other questions to keep probing. Resist the temptation to insert your own opinions, which will tend to shut down the conversation. If you begin to work with these individuals in a coaching relationship, you will later see how the attitudes they express here carry over to shape their behavior.

Linda presented a true coaching challenge. She was a veteran financial advisor of 12 years and chronically plateaued. In her mind, she always set goals. But she also loved to say, "My goals aren't necessarily what my firm wants me to do." That statement was an important clue into her state of mind.

She was basically negative toward anything that pushed her outside her comfort zone. She had nearly a thousand clients, over 120 million dollars in assets, but was producing less than $500,000. Any discussion about streamlining her book, hiring a junior financial advisor, or transitioning more to managed money was met with a cold stare and a negative comment about her firm. She recently said to her current manager, "You're my eighth manager in 12 years. Soon you'll be gone. The firm will either promote you or fire you, and I'll still be the person who has to answer to my clients." You could clearly hear how she rationalized her negative attitudes.

When the discussion focused on delivering more value to her clients by adding more services, Linda was more open. She had a Master's Degree in Education and was proud of her intellectual capabilities. So that became the focus of our initial FastTrack Coaching relationship with her. She knew that in order to learn, a person had to change. She also recognized that we are all creatures of habit, and that in order to change, a person has to break certain habits. She would even talk openly about needing to go outside her comfort zone.

Our ground rules with Linda were simple; focus only on what she could directly control. Period! No firm bashing or disparaging manager comments. All her cognitive efforts were to be directed toward delivering more value to her clients and making her business more efficient.

Without realizing it, Linda had agreed to change aspects of her behavioral and attitudinal patterns. She stopped her defensive reaction toward improving her business by no longer getting into manager or firm issues. Since they were outside her control, this made sense to her. Behaviorally, she hired a part-time assistant to help her begin to contact and service all of her households more effectively.

At first glance, it doesn't appear that Linda is doing much of anything other than complaining less. But from a coaching perspective, she has taken a major step forward. She is changing some very specific habits.

Linda is not a poster-child for coaching, but no one is. She is not someone her firm would invite to their training center to share her story. But Linda is a success story in her own right. Twenty-four months later, she had given 300 clients to a young financial advisor of her choosing (her idea), and had created a small team comprised of herself and a licensed full-time assistant. Her licensed assistant was handling all the middle tier and smaller accounts. Linda's production has now grown to slightly north of $700,000.

Wealth is largely a result of habit.

JOHN JACOB ASTOR

None of this would have occurred without a change in habits. And once she got rid of the verbal defenses for maintaining her status quo, Linda didn't need much coaching. We left her with our 21st Century Financial Practice tool kit after explaining how to use only the processes that fit her needs. She did the rest.

HABIT

I am your constant companion.
I am your greatest helper or heaviest burden.
I will push you onward or drag you down to failure.
I am completely at your command.
Half of the things you do, you might just as well turn over to me,
and I will be able to do them quickly and correctly.

I am easily managed – you must merely be firm with me.
Show me exactly how you want something done,
and after a few lessons, I will do it automatically.
I am the servant of all great people;
and alas, of all failures as well.
Those who are great, I have made great.
Those who are failures, I have made failures.

I am not a machine,
though I work with all the precision of a machine
plus the intelligence of a human.
You may run me for a profit or run me for ruin —
it makes no difference to me.

Take me, train me, be firm with me,
and I will place the world at your feet.
Be easy with me, and I will destroy you.

Who Am I? I Am Habit!

Anonymous

CHAPTER 7

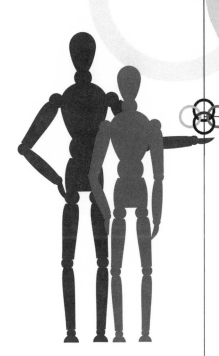

GOALS AND MOTIVATION

Show me a thoroughly satisfied man and I will show you a failure.

THOMAS EDISON

Every response you make is determined by what you think you are and what you want to be. What you want to be must determine every response you make.

A COURSE IN MIRACLES

Goals establish direction. As Yogi Berra so aptly put it, "If you don't know where you're going, you could wind up someplace else." One of the greatest challenges you face, as a coach, is to help people set, pursue, and achieve goals. It seems so simple, so logical, that you might expect this to be your easiest task. But it won't be, and here are some of the reasons.

- Most people do not set goals properly. Yet, everyone is goal driven – if not by their own goals, by someone else's. The organizational structures we create and management styles we typically use place most people in the position of being driven by goals other than their own.

- When driven by someone else's goals, a person must constantly change direction to meet the needs of someone else. If you are driven by your goals, your life is focused. You understand what it means to be an achiever.

- Even when the opportunity is there, many resist setting goals. One reason is the fear of failure. If you don't set goals, you can't be held accountable for achieving them.

- Rejection is another reason for not setting goals. There is always someone waiting to tell us that we can't possibly achieve the goals we have set.

- When goals are not properly established, they can be brutally de-motivating. That is why so many people are reluctant to even set goals. However, when goals are used correctly, they light the internal fires of self-motivation and achievement drive.

The irony here is profound. In the retail world of financial services, every trainee is taught to set goals. In many cases, they have to meet quotas in order to keep their jobs. Whether they're called quotas or goals, the end game is to keep financial advisors motivated to market and sell financial products and services.

The manager's role in this end game is prominent, especially when he or she has a financial interest in the success or failure of the trainees. Managers are taught to help financial advisors set goals, complete an annual business plan, and review their progress with the assumption that this will produce the desired results. But something seems to be missing. With all the hoopla regarding goals and business plans, why is it that so few financial advisors and teams are truly goal focused? Why are so few doing specific fixed daily activities that are linked to a desired goal or quota?

Attempts to answer those questions often take us in circles, creating another set of questions. Do goals motivate, or do people have to be motivated to set and achieve goals? Why does there seem to be so much goal resistance in tough times when setting and achieving goals are more important than ever?

PROBABILITY OF SUCCESS

To find answers that make sense, we turn to the research by two esteemed psychologists, David C. McClelland of Harvard and John Atkinson of the University of Michigan. They emphasize that the key to breaking through the goal resistance barrier is *perceived probability of success.*

According to McClelland and Atkinson, motivation strength is at its peak (100%) when we believe there is about a 50% probability that we can achieve our goals.

- We **do not** become self-motivated toward goal achievement when the probability of goal success is either *virtually certain* (100%) or *virtually impossible* to attain (0%).

- Translated, that also means that the people you coach will not become self-motivated by unrealistic expectations (quotas) of their manager. In fact, failure to meet unrealistically high managerial expectations typically leads to high rates of attrition, both voluntary and involuntary.

McClelland and Atkinson's research suggests that the greatest level of motivation will occur when an individual perceives a 50 percent probability of success in achieving a specific goal. Whenever the probability of success is much less than that, people tend to psychologically give up as soon as they determine their goal is unattainable.

You might expect this of a rookie, but even veterans are falling into this trap as they get excited about building a 21st Century Financial Practice and commit to attracting more affluent relationships than is realistic. Why? Because they truly do not understand what is involved. When the individuals and teams you are going to coach look at the gaps that exist between where they are now and where they want to go, they need to have confidence that they can close that gap. An important role of your coaching is to help clarify the action steps required to close that gap. Increased goal clarity will also help to increase the probability of goal success.

*There is no man living who isn't capable of doing
more than he thinks he can do.*

HENRY FORD

SETTING GOALS

Conversely, there is little fuel for those motivational juices if the goals being set are set too low. This is a common mistake of many veteran financial advisors. In order to protect their ego, there is an inherent distaste for anything that suggests possible failure. Consequently many veteran financial advisors have developed the habit of creating an annual business plan that they can comfortably expect to achieve. These financial advisors are chronically plateaued and have very low achievement drive. Because their goals have such a high probability of goal success, there is nothing there to motivate them and they resist anything that resembles change.

The fact that only five percent of the 200 wealth management team members we surveyed said that they were highly goal focused, suggests how potent this factor of goal motivation can be. Targeting the affluent happens only when it becomes a highly desired goal. Which is exactly why a coach is needed. Jim and Larry's story is a perfect example.

It was back in the early nineties, and I had just finished our second of six sessions in an Achiever Group coaching format that I was facilitating (see Chapter 13). All the financial advisors had established quantum growth goals during our first session, and during the second session I paired them off into working partners to further strengthen their accountability.

Jim and Larry opted to be working partners – and then decided to go one step further. They had just formed a wealth management team and wanted to hire me to serve as their personal coach. Both were transactional financial advisors who wanted to transition into managed money and focus on raising assets. "What's your goal?" I asked. They responded, "Currently we have 80 million in assets, and we want to have 100 million." My response caught them by surprise, "I'm not interested."

They were incredulous! Here I was facilitating this Achiever Group of 12 financial advisors and was turning them down. "We're going to pay your going rate," explained Jim. Again I told them, "No."

Needless to say, they couldn't figure it out – until I shared the McClelland-Atkinson research with the entire group. At that point I turned to Jim and Larry and asked, "How much of a stretch is it for you guys to go from 80 to 100 million in assets?" They both admitted, not much.

When I mentioned that 200 million in assets would be a target that would get my attention, they both turned pale. But they agreed, and again asked me to coach them. Within 18 months, they had 225 million in assets and at this writing they manage close to a billion dollars.

The reason I initially refused to coach Jim and Larry was somewhat self-serving because I didn't want to waste my time or theirs. Setting a target with total assurance that they could achieve it meant that neither was likely to venture outside his respective comfort zone. Yes, they might achieve their low goal; but I knew that little if any change would occur and I would be a frustrated coach. By simply applying the McClelland and Atkinson goal motivation principle, I was able to push them outside their comfort zones where they were forced to change. They knew that I would not allow them to shirk from working hard to achieve the goals they had set, and they have been thanking me ever since.

*People with goals succeed
because they know where they're going.*

EARL NIGHTINGALE

Not meaning to sound redundant, but let me say it once more, one of the greatest challenges you face is encouraging and helping the individuals and teams you coach to set, pursue, and achieve goals that truly ignite self-motivational fires. Fortunately, the FastTrack Coaching process naturally incorporates this form of goal setting into the Action Agreement process covered in Chapters 4 and 5.

The purpose of this chapter is to help you understand the vital relationship between goals and motivation – and prepare you for any resistance you might encounter. For each individual and team you coach, the big question will be, what is their *perceived probability of success* for the goals they set in order to close the gap between where they are now and where they need to be in order to successfully attract, service, and retain affluent investors?

Exploring McClelland and Atkinson's work and applying their principles can initially be very uncomfortable for managers, trainers, and coaches. Why? Perhaps because much like the financial advisors they work with, they too have been conditioned to evaluate success in the shallow context of whether or not a goal that was set can be easily achieved. Often there is the additional pressure of financial incentives attached to these accomplishments, so setting goals that have a perceived 50 percent probability of success makes them nervous.

That is why the first coaching Action Agreement focuses exclusively on completing the 5-year business plan. Developing that agreement and later reviewing what has been accomplished will tell you a lot about the *perceived probability of success* – and provide helpful clues about the challenges that lie ahead.

People do not achieve because they set easy goals. The key is to begin with a realistically challenging goal, and then apply what I consider to be the most important element of human psychology – the Achievement Cycle, which we will cover in Chapter 8.

CHAPTER 8

THE ACHIEVEMENT CYCLE

There are two pains in life, the pain of discipline, and the pain of regret.
UNKNOWN

Perhaps the most valuable result of all education is the ability to make yourself do the thing you have to do, when it ought to be done, whether you like it or not.
THOMAS H. HUXLEY

Coaching impact points present themselves in every possible size, shape, and flavor when you have trustworthy tools for ferreting out fact from fiction and getting people back on track. The more time you spend coaching, the more fiction (or excuses) you will encounter. Such was the case when I shared an elevator ride with a financial advisor who is a partner in one of the larger teams in his branch.

"Boy it's tiring when you're fielding calls all day from clients who are upset because we didn't get them out of Enron at 80," said Jerry after exchanging pleasantries. "I find myself going home totally wiped out."

From that one statement, I suspected that neither Jerry nor any other member of his team was actively doing anything to develop new high quality business. So I decided to find out and asked, "What are you doing to attract prospects that fit your ideal client profile?" Jerry frowned and replied, "I know you think we should be meeting with our clients and generating referrals, but I have to tell you, it's very difficult to ask someone for a referral when they are mad at you for losing their money. We've decided to put all new business development on hold until we clean up all this mess with our clients."

Well, by the time we got out of the elevator Jerry was on his cell phone trying to get his two partners to meet with us. What did I do to stimulate that kind of reaction? It was simple. I empathized with their plight, and then I stated firmly that the real reason they were not bringing in any new business is that they had simply let their achievement cycle go on vacation. I told him that the most expedient way to pull themselves out of their malaise, and not feel so devastated, was for each of them to *do something* every day to bring in new business – regardless of how they felt.

When I met with the team later in the day, they had already discussed what they needed to do. All they really needed from me was to acknowledge and confirm their renewed commitment. I took a few moments to review the *Achievement Cycle* concept and point out that they were far too proud and successful to not be engaged in that cycle every day.

My time spent with that team was only about 15 minutes, but my coaching impact point had been made in the elevator. Because I understood the role of doing the activities necessary to reach a goal, regardless of what one is thinking or feeling, it was easy for me to sense that this team was disengaged from the *Achievement Cycle*. Everything else builds upon it. They were pros and knew what they needed to do once the point was made. The *Achievement Cycle* is an amazing, yet simple tool that can get anyone immediately on track.

Below are the two *achievement cycles* that were exemplified in the case I just shared with you. It may not be easy to see the difference at first glance, which illustrates why people often think that they are goal focused when they are not. But look carefully. There is a difference – and it's very significant.

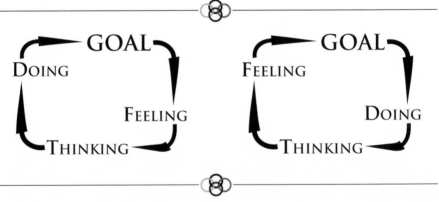

An illustration is Bill Jones, who is feeling those Monday morning blues. "I'm not really up to making that referral call this morning. I think I'll _____ instead." (You fill in the blank.)

Bill Jones is experiencing the Achievement Cycle on the left. Actually, it's a *non-achievement cycle*. He is allowing his negative *feelings* to impact his *thinking* so he can come up with an excuse to *do* something else that is not as "uncomfortable." He will be much less productive than he should and could be today.

If you were going to coach Bill Jones, your challenge would be to guide and direct him toward the *real* Achievement Cycle on the right. Notice that it begins with *doing*, which is almost completely under his control! That is how you break out of your comfort zone – *by doing*.

After observing the financial salespeople he had managed for years, Albert E. N. Gray told his 1940 NALU Convention audience, "The common denominator of success – the secret of success of every man who has ever been successful – lies in the fact that he formed the habit of doing things that failures don't like to do." The only change that I would make to his statement would be to make it gender inclusive, because the wisdom of it is timeless for all of us!

We have established that people tend to do what they think. Actually, what really blocks people from achieving is getting caught up in **The Non-Achievement Cycle**. Note the sequence: *Feeling* → *Thinking* → *Doing*.

When feelings emerge from our subconscious, they shape our thinking and ultimately impact what we do. Negative feelings cause us to find excuses to not do what we know deep down inside we should do. Those feelings help us to remain in our comfort zone. Only the purest of positive feelings can strengthen our thinking to the extent that we will do exactly what we should do.

Whereas in **The Achievement Cycle**, the sequence changes to:
Doing → *Thinking* → *Feeling*.

Doing is the key to successful performance. The non-Achievement Cycle becomes the Achievement Cycle when a person reverses by doing first – thinking about what was achieved second – and then feeling good about the success third. Doing is almost completely under a person's control. That's how to break out of a Comfort Zone – by doing! Doing, despite any setbacks, results in achievement. Achievement creates positive thinking, which causes us to feel good. The achievement, positive thinking, and good feelings are transferred to our subconscious mind and stored for later positive reinforcement.

My family gets annoyed whenever I share this experience, but since it so clearly illustrates the powerful influence of the doing-thinking-feeling Achievement Cycle they are willing to grin and bear it.

The story took place a number of years ago when Heidi, our oldest of three, was a Brownie and came home one January evening all excited about selling Girl Scout cookies. "Daddy! Daddy! It's Girl Scout cookie time and I've got to sell 100 boxes to win a prize. We've got to go out now and sell Girl Scout cookies." Yes, anyone who's ever had a Girl Scout in the family understands about the 'we' in cookie sales.

Heidi had a goal. She wanted to sell 100 boxes of Girl Scout cookies. The next thing I knew Heidi's younger sister Amy, our golden retriever Gypsy, and I were walking around the block. The girls knocked on the doors, Gypsy and I waited at the curb, and 1½ hours later, we arrived home cold and hungry for a late dinner, with only 16 boxes sold. But Heidi was still excited.

Two nights later, I returned from a speaking engagement and found Heidi sitting at the kitchen table with a pout on her face. She blurted out, "Daddy it's not fair! Two of the girls' parents are selling cookies at work, and they've already sold 65 and 75 boxes! There's no way I can win. So I want you to take my cookie list and sell cookies at your next speech." Ouch!

My best efforts at persuading her on the merits of doing this herself fell on deaf ears. It was only after we took a long walk with Gypsy that I stumbled on a way to keep her engaged in doing what she needed to do. "What if we kept your goal of selling 100 boxes, but instead of a troop prize, you would win my prize of a dinner for just the two of us anywhere you like."

Heidi thought for a moment and then stated firmly, "Okay. But you're going to take me for a pizza dinner whether you eat pizza or not." A deal was struck, and she continued to do what was necessary, eventually selling 102 boxes.

Was her thinking positive as she again pursued her goal with this new incentive of a pizza dinner with Dad? Not really. She was still angry with the other girls who she thought were cheating, their parents, and me for refusing to sell cookies at my speeches. How did she feel about the entire affair? Not good. Her standard line was, "It's not fair." Then how did she achieve her original goal and sell those 102 boxes? She did it by doing it – and then thinking about what she was achieving and why (to support a program that she enjoyed) – and then discovering that she felt really good about the experience. Giving up because of what someone else was doing was replaced by doing it for the right reasons and feeling good about it.

This little incident illustrates why the doing-thinking-feeling progression of the Achievement Cycle is so important. When pursuing an important goal, it's easy to become distracted by what's going on around us and then allowing that to influence our feelings, which in turn distorts our thinking, and ultimately has us doing something else.

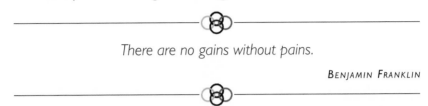

There are no gains without pains.

BENJAMIN FRANKLIN

PATTERN OF ACHIEVEMENT

Establishing the doing-thinking-feeling cycle of achievement is what starts us in the right direction. But what keeps us on track? How can we maintain that cycle throughout, ensuring that we will ultimately achieve our goal?

That answer can also be found in Heidi's experience. The "pattern of achievement" was established in the beginning, when Heidi, Amy, Gypsy and I walked around the block and eventually sold 16 boxes of cookies, which led to Heidi's excitement. After dealing with Heidi's frustrations and providing a new incentive, we returned to that pattern. She also sold boxes on her own, and established a pattern for doing that. Doing doesn't occur in a haphazard way. We establish a pattern, refine it until it works well, and then continue that pattern until our goal is achieved – as you will see in the following exercise.

Think back over your past and select two *achievements* that have given you a sense of pride. As you place yourself back in the role of doing what needed to be done, recall your thoughts; even that devilish voice of doubt. Re-visit your feelings as you forced yourself outside your comfort zone to do what was necessary. After this pleasant journey into your past, complete the chart on the next page with information about each achievement.

- "**Achievements No. 1 and No. 2**" – describe each achievement.

- "**ACTIVITIES**" – list the specific tasks and on-going activities you had to do in order to complete each achievement.

- "**Pattern of USE**" – state how often you did each task and activity. Was it only one time, daily, weekly?

- Then go back to your list of "**ACTIVITIES**" and place a check mark in front of each one that you believe was essential to your success.

PATTERN OF ACHIEVEMENT	
ACTIVITIES	PATTERN OF USE (ONCE, DAILY, WEEKLY, ETC.)
Achievement No. 1...	
Achievement No. 2...	

What this exercise demonstrates is the power of *doing*. It was not the desiring of the achievement that made you successful. It was *doing* the tasks and activities – according to the pattern you established, that brought about the success.

After completing the *Benchmarking Your Future* assessment tool, financial advisors are encouraged to map out their next steps. The first step is to rank their performance gaps to determine where to begin. Gap analysis, diagrammed below, is the second step, and this is where the Achievement Cycle needs to really "kick in."

PRESENT SITUATION		DESIRED OUTCOME
Why this performance **gap** exists.	**Action Steps** to close the performance gap.	What it will look like when I have closed this performance gap. Target Date:

PRESENT SITUATION

Have them describe in specific terms why this performance gap exists. The more honest and specific they are, the greater success they will have in closing the gap. This is a positive and necessary exercise because they will only move ahead when they understand clearly where they are now. Don't get into a discussion about why they should do this. Just tell them, "Trust me, this is important."

DESIRED OUTCOME

Have them describe what they want to have "in place" when they have successfully eliminated the performance gap. Encourage them not to worry about how they are going to get there, but simply describe what "there" will look like. Again, they will need to trust you, because this too is important.

ACTION STEPS

Closing the gap can seem overwhelming. The key is to define and sequence the steps they need to take to close the gap. Don't worry about a long list, or even an exact list. The key is to establish the first two or three things they *need to do* to get started. As they successfully complete each step, they will begin to think and feel good things. Step-by-step-by-step they will perform better and better. Before they know it, achieving the 21st Century Financial Practice will be just around the corner.

Using the performance gap model helps to clarify the task ahead, but closing the gap remains the real challenge. For some, it will seem to be an overwhelming challenge, because the gap between the old Wall Street sales and marketing model and the 21st Century Financial Practice model represents a significant change. The chart on the next page illustrates the difference.

This entire section on Individual Performance is arguably the most important aspect of FastTrack Coaching. The better you understand basic human psychology, and are able to personalize this knowledge to each individual you coach, the greater impact you will have on helping them succeed.

You make up your mind before you start that
sacrifice is part of the package.

RICH DEVOS

The **Achievement Cycle** is the heart of all your coaching efforts. Your objective as a FastTrack coach is to activate the Achievement Cycle of everyone you are coaching. If you are unable to get someone to do the specific activities that are linked to a goal, regardless of what they might be thinking or how they might feel, you will not be much help to them.

Wall Street Sales & Marketing Model	21st Century Financial Practice Model
Target anyone with money to invest.	Target specific categories of affluent investors.
Achieve quarterly/yearly production goals.	Incrementally achieve a 5-year business plan
Measure only what you've already achieved.	Measure weekly indicators of future success.
Use cold calls, references and other means to contact and attract prospective clients.	Network for introductions and referrals.
Sell investment transactions.	Qualify and close long-term clients.
Specialize in mutual funds, stocks, and other investments.	Provide solutions in eight financial areas.
Pick up the phone and sell.	Guide clients through a 6-step advisory process.
Operate alone with an assistant or two.	Function as part of a wealth management team.
Delegate tasks as needed.	Organize team member areas of responsibility.
Talk with your assistant(s) as needed.	Conduct effective team meetings.
Spend most of your time getting new clients.	Upgrade clients and build client loyalty.

Every action agreement serves to engage the Achievement Cycle. The role of the FastTrack coach is really threefold:

1. Activate the Achievement Cycle

2. Make certain the right activities are being done the right way

3. Keep the Achievement Cycle activated

Obviously, your role as a coach is more complex than this, but simple concepts are often the foundation for sustained growth and personal development. If you keep your coaching simple, and make certain everyone you coach is **doing**, you can help them overcome any negatives that exist and put them on the FastTrack to success.

Knowing is not enough, we must apply.
Willing is not enough, we must do.

JOHANN WOLFGANG VON GOETHE

Mastering this concept will keep you and the people you coach from falling into the "getting ready to get ready" trap that is prevalent in business coaching. Some people love to get involved with theory, planning, and classroom work, but avoid going outside of their comfort zone to do the activities necessary to achieve a quantifiable goal. FastTrack coaching them to remain in the *Achievement Cycle* compels them to transform all their intellectual development into experiential reality.

COACHING
TEAMS

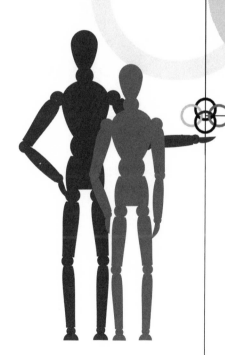

CHAPTER 9

WHY TEAMS

Great teamwork is the only way we create the breakthroughs that define our careers.

PAT RILEY

The most effective way to forge a winning team is to call on the players to connect with something larger than themselves...to surrender their self-interest for the greater good so that the whole adds up to more than the sum of the parts.

PHIL JACKSON

Recently I listened to a senior executive of a major wirehouse speaking at his firm's national branch managers meeting. He made an interesting comparison between spelling "cat" and "chrysanthemum" to drive home his point about the magnitude of current changes impacting the world of financial services.

> When I first got my license as a registered rep, our training was about as basic as learning how to spell 'cat'. So we all learned how to spell 'cat', and our clients expected us only to be able to spell 'cat'. Today our financial advisors must be able to spell 'chrysanthemum' just to compete. 'Cat' is not enough. Our challenge as a management team is to make certain all of our financial advisors can spell 'chrysanthemum'.

I'm not doing his speech justice, but the message is clear: it was simpler back then – it's far more complicated now. Bingo! Very few financial advisors, if any, are going to be able to meet the expectations of their affluent clientele working alone. They need help. Whether it is an indispensable assistant, a practice manager, or additional financial advisors with complimenting expertise; the reality is that no one person can deliver what is expected in today's world. Spelling 'chrysanthemum' is too hard for one person; it takes a team.

Back in the days of spelling 'cat', brokers would hear, "I have about $10,000 to invest, and I'm wondering if I should put it in mutual funds, dabble some in the stock market, or use it to expand my IRA. What do you suggest?" That is the kind of solution the stockbroker or financial advisor of yesteryear had to be ready to provide; it didn't require much assistance to spell 'cat'.

Compare that with today's affluent investor who has considerably more investable assets with his or her own unique set of financial priorities and goals that may include any of the following:

• Meet current financial obligations to creditors.

• Reduce debt that cannot be paid off in the current month.

- Eliminate debt within ___ months.

- Maintain or upgrade personal life-style.

- Provide for personal financial security, enabling them to never be reliant on others.

- Have an ongoing understanding of their net worth.

- Budget what they have coming in and how they use it.

- Minimize the amount of taxes they pay, and pay those taxes on time.

- Insure against serious financial loss due to medical bills and/or not being able to work.

- Insure against serious financial loss from having to replace or repair damage to their home, other real estate, vehicles, and other large tangible property investments.

- Pay for the present education of adult family members and the future education of children.

- Retire by age ___.

- Retire with at least ___% of their current level of income for at least ___ years.

- Have a detailed plan of how and to whom their property, valuables, and money will be distributed upon their death(s).

- Have a charitable giving plan that is consistent with their values and compatible with the rest of their financial needs, goals, and priorities.

As you read the above list, you probably found yourself piecing together the letters to spell 'chrysanthemum.' There are at least eight or nine definable financial service categories including budgeting and cash flow management, insurance, investments, taxes, education, and estate planning.

Now, imagine a solo financial advisor meeting with each client to determine which items are priorities and the specific goals they have for each. Then imagine that same advisor taking those priorities and goals, developing a written financial plan and helping each client select and secure the right financial products. Then again, imagine the advisor interacting with each client at appropriate points in time in order to help each one manage those priorities and achieve their goals. No financial advisor, not even one with a great assistant, could take care of all that on their own!

It is always your next move.

NAPOLEON HILL

Because it takes a team, your coaching will often have a team focus. Your team coaching efforts will be divided between coaching individual team members (particularly the team leader) and working with the team as a whole. It may even be necessary to coach two or more team members who are working on a specific aspect of the team's development. In this chapter we will help you to recognize and understand some key team dynamics and find ways to coach more effectively when working in a team setting.

WHEN A TEAM IS NOT!

None of this information has been lost on today's financial advisor. The idea of "teams" is a hot topic; almost a fad. Financial advisors are frantically searching for teammates, while managers work hard to be matchmakers. This is not a good recipe for long-term success!

As a FastTrack coach, it's important for you to make certain that your financial advisors form teams the right way, for the right reasons, and especially with the right people. Our first basic commandment of successful teams is that they must be properly conceived.

You will want to know exactly why the team was formed, what each team member brings to the table, and how they envision blending their collective experience and expertise to meet the multidimensional needs of affluent clients. There must be no hidden agendas!

A *team* truly becomes a team when they focus on collective performance that is shaped by a common purpose with shared goals to achieve. Effective teams use a unified and disciplined approach to decision-making and thrive on mutual accountability. That will only happen if the team is properly conceived and every individual is saying, "Let's get serious about becoming a legitimate wealth management team."

As you look at the teams you will be coaching, you may recognize examples of the following levels of teams.

LEVEL 1

"I'll just get me an assistant or two to relieve my work load."

Although this level is slowly being eradicated, we do still see evidence of this approach in many places. The following situation will reveal what can happen within a Level 1 team.

A client wants to open an IRA on April 15. The client's financial advisor says that he will be out of the office and the client should ask for his assistant or junior partner. When the client walks in at 3 p.m. on April 15, the assistant has no idea why, as the client hands the blank forms (with signature only) to her. When the assistant asks the client for the missing information, the client says he doesn't have it with him. His financial advisor had told him to just sign it, and his assistant would do the rest.

In a Level 1 team, assistants often complain that they only do menial tasks such as filing, answering the phone, and getting coffee for their boss; a tell-tale sign of a financial practice bogged down with too many clients. Uninformed and unprepared team members are often called upon to handle a vast array of client issues when the senior financial advisor is out of the office.

Anyone who insists on operating in this way is probably not a valid candidate for building a wealth management team capable of attracting, servicing, and retaining affluent clients.

Level 2

"We can cover for each other, help each other, and market ourselves as a team."

We refer to this as a collective grouping, and it is usually done for the wrong reasons; such as covering for each other when on vacation or sharing the expense of support staff. Some may consider it to be a good marketing strategy, hoping that "team selling" will assist them in closing larger accounts. These financial advisors may sincerely intend to function as a team but cannot seem to integrate their efforts. They continue as individuals, selling and handling clients in the same one-dimensional manner as before.

Level 2 teams like the idea of being a team, but the team itself is not properly conceived. Although the team members are experienced in selling intangibles, and often highly skilled, those skills will be ineffective when it comes to affluent investors. Meanwhile the team members, their managers, their firms, and their peers, may perceive them as a team that just needs to put forth more effort at teamwork. Nothing could be further from the truth. Because the team was not conceived properly, there is no unified purpose, no shared goals, no unified and disciplined approach to decision-making, and no mutual accountability.

Level 3

"The Company wants us to form a team."

This is a mistake often made when a company recognizes that it takes a team to meet the multidimensional financial needs of affluent investors. However, teams formed by a company mandate are too often improperly conceived. The team members need to have their own reasons to form a team, and each team member must agree on those reasons. Even then, they will have to work very hard to make it work, because the members did not initiate the formation of the team.

Forming a Level 1, Level 2 or Level 3 team does not a team make! In such cases, individuals who are used to working independently have been brought together, but they continue to focus on individual performance. Closely guarding their own turf, they limit decision making to those things that enable each individual to do his or her job better. They may even attend some team training, but will tend to leave most of what is presented to them back in the training room, and return to their offices to continue business as usual.

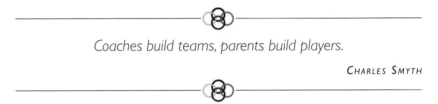

Coaches build teams, parents build players.

CHARLES SMYTH

COACHING THE TRANSFORMATION TO A LEVEL 4 TEAM

When you encounter Level 2 and Level 3 teams, institute your coaching effort by having them "disband mentally" so that in their mind they are starting all over again. Then bring them together and explain the "properly conceived" principle to them. Place the key elements in the form of the following questions on a flip chart and on paper that you distribute to each person.

- Why should we form a team?

- What do we each bring to this team?

- How do we envision blending our collective experience and expertise to meet the multidimensional needs of affluent clients?

- What, if any, hidden agendas do we need to be aware of?

- How can we make certain that we do not become a sales group posturing as a wealth management practice?

You ask the questions – but let them give and discuss the answers. Listen carefully and make certain that they are on their way to becoming a Level 4 team before you agree to coach them.

The first **FastTrack Coaching Action Agreement** you will develop with those you coach (as discussed in Chapter 5) focuses on creating a 5-year business plan. This is a good place to begin a discussion on teams – it may be about forming a team, realigning an existing team, or simply improving upon what is already working well.

Before investing the time to meet with a team, it is best to sit down with the team leader (usually the largest producer) to get a buy-in to the entire process. Although the team leader may have already passed the muster to enter into a coaching relationship by completing the pre-coaching form and Benchmarking tool, you are often dealing with fairly large egos. I have seen team leaders react very defensively in front of their teams when dealing with gaps uncovered through the Benchmarking tool.

However, these same team leaders often behave quite differently when discussing sensitive issues privately with the coach. It's similar to a parent defending a child's behavior in public when questioned, whereas in private such behavior would not be tolerated. It's one of those funny quirks in human nature, but one that can save you a lot of time and consternation once you understand it.

Following is just one of many examples of what can go wrong when meeting with a team without taking the time to meet privately with the team leader in advance.

Mary sat down with her largest team for a Saturday morning, first time coaching session. They had completed the Benchmarking Tool and discovered a number of gaps. Mary knew the dynamics of the team: a father and son who did not get along and two assistants, one siding with the father and the other with the son. Communication was horrible. Profanity and tears were not uncommon. Mary wondered how the father had built such a successful business.

Three hours later, Mary decided to terminate the coaching relationship. Someone, and not always the same someone, had stubbornly contested every issue. Mary felt as though they had circled the wagons to hold off anyone who would attempt to coach them.

Obviously, there is no guarantee that Mary would ever have had a successful coaching relationship with this father-son team. But by meeting first with the team leader, in this case the father, she would have definitely increased her chances.

In most cases, the team leader, who is often the senior financial advisor, should complete the initial Action Agreement. The meeting with the team leader, prior to the meeting with the entire team, can serve as a discovery phase outside the official coaching relationship. It is not unusual to uncover some delicate personnel issues that people were not previously aware of, in these pre-coaching meetings; issues that probably would not have surfaced in an official team coaching session.

Not every team you coach will have been properly conceived according to the factors listed above. That's reality. Your challenge as a coach is to understand how teams tend to develop and what you can do to coach them most effectively.

CHAPTER 10

THE FOUR STAGES OF TEAM DEVELOPMENT

Coming together is a beginning; keeping together is progress; working together is success.

HENRY FORD

The best teams have chemistry. They communicate with each other and they sacrifice personal glory for the common good.

DAVE DEBUSSCHERE

After investing a lot of time and energy in coaching the formation of a team, there is a tendency to step back and allow the team to develop on its own. Especially when you have a group that is beginning to emerge as a Level 4 team. All is well, right? Maybe so today, but it will not last, and there's a good reason.

Ever since Elton Mayo of Harvard discovered the impact of small groups on productivity during his famous Hawthorne Studies in 1924, teams and teamwork have played a vital role in shaping organizational success. That gives us a history of more than 75 years to help us understand what makes a team effective.

One valuable lesson we have learned is that teams go through predictable stages of development. That predictability benefits you as a coach in several ways.

- **First**, there are no surprises. You know what to expect and can better anticipate and recognize the bumps and jolts when they come.

- **Second**, you know that others have experienced those same bumps and jolts – and that they were able to work through them. Therefore the team you are coaching can as well.

- **Third**, you can help the teams you coach prepare for a smoother transition as they move from one stage to the other – as long as you know what to look for and what to do.

There are essentially four stages of team development that have had different labels applied to them over the years. We will use the wonderfully descriptive ones popularized by Joiner Associates: *Forming, Storming, Norming* and *Performing*.

The following descriptions will tell you what to expect and what you, as their coach, can do to help your teams move from one stage to the next.

Stage 1

Forming

There are two distinct variations of the *Forming Stage*.

- A new team – individuals come together to form a new team.

- An existing team – team members are ready to shift their focus toward targeting the affluent.

In each case, your first coaching challenge is to guide the team through six vital **Forming Stage development tasks**.

1. Create a written 5-year business plan (Action Agreement 1).

2. Establish their metrics scorecards (Action Agreement 2).

3. Delegate areas of responsibility to individual team members (Action Agreement 10).

4. Clarify the fixed daily activities that drive the areas of responsibility (Action Agreement 10).

5. Evaluate each team member's past production trends and project their future in light of the team's new direction (see Chapter 11).

6. Use the trend and projection analysis to formulate a fair and motivating compensation plan for all team members (see Chapter 11).

A wise man will make more opportunities than he finds.

Francis Bacon

You will likely encounter what we refer to as a coaching "aha" when helping teams through these key tasks. The importance of each task is obvious for members of new teams. Members of existing teams however, may not see the value of the tasks. But, do not be swayed because of their resistance. All teams are in desperate need of being coached through the *Forming Stage* despite any temptation to rush through it.

The tendency for existing teams is to assume that they are already in the *Performing Stage*. But they are mistaken. Each *Forming Stage* development task previously described will likely produce an "aha" from you, as well as the team members, as you uncover issues that need attention.

Although many will try to give the impression of independence, most team members arrive at this stage feeling very dependent. This is true of new teams as well as existing teams going through a major transformation.

Members of *new teams* will be wondering how (or if) they will fit into this team. Questions going through their minds might include: Will I feel like an insider or outsider? Do I want to belong? Who's calling the shots? Will I have influence? Will I be heard? How can I contribute? Will we all get along?

Questions that have previously been avoided often surface among members of *existing teams*, such as: What is our real business plan? What are my delegated areas of responsibility? How will my contribution be measured – and compensated? Can I really speak my mind?

This is when team leadership is needed, to pull everyone together. If you are coaching an existing team through this stage, you might find it useful to have the team members complete the *Team Self-Assessment* tool. You will find a copy at the end of this chapter. The most important thing you can do as a team coach is to prepare the team leader to guide the team through this stage.

DETERMINING THE TEAM MODEL

Before getting very far into coaching a team, it is a good idea for everyone to agree upon the Team Model (structure). Essentially there are four basic models to follow in shaping a wealth management team. You will find a detailed description of these team models in Chapter 11.

Vertical Team Model One – Senior team member, rookie junior team member, support personnel, and specialists.

Vertical Team Model Two – Senior team member, experienced junior team member, support personnel, and specialists.

Vertical Team Model Three – Senior team member, support personnel, and specialists.

Horizontal Team Model – Two or more senior team members, support personnel, and specialists.

Determining the team model in the Forming Stage helps to clarify roles and establish personal goals. Use the descriptions in Chapter 11 to help eliminate any confusion over the structure of the group.

You may face an occasion where your most difficult challenge will be to help two financial advisors create a functional Horizontal Team. Laura's story highlights why a manager who lacked coaching skills, could have easily thrown up his or her hands and walked away.

Laura was a 600 thousand dollar producer with 130 million dollars in assets and 740 households in her book. She loved her clients, worked extremely hard (almost to the point of burnout) and was tremendous at developing relationships with serious money. She could attract affluent investors into her practice, but she had a time problem. For the past three years she had been stuck in her office servicing existing clients.

Donald, a friend of Laura's for 15 years, had entered the financial services business at the same time as Laura. They trusted each other completely and had complementary skills. Donald was a detail person who loved to create sophisticated plans for people with serious money and then handle every aspect of their financial affairs. He too was a 600 thousand dollar producer, but his assets were only 60 million dollars from only 150 households.

Despite Donald's low asset total, it seemed like a great match. He could organize Laura's existing clients, do the planning, and transition more assets to fee and Laura could concentrate on developing new affluent relationships.

They had discussed forming a team for nearly two years, but neither seemed able to get off the dime. Both had been sole practitioners for so long and had witnessed so many teams break up that they were afraid to act. But now as they talked seriously, it basically boiled down to two issues: growth and compensation. Laura thought she was giving too much away at a fifty-fifty split since she had more than twice Donald's assets. Donald was only interested in teaming-up if it was fifty-fifty and he could have access to Laura's clients.

Their manager helped bring this to closure when he met with them and used our 21st Century Forecaster to help them see, in quantifiable terms, what was possible. If Donald annuitized a certain portion of Laura's book; and if Laura brought in one new affluent relationship per month; they calculated that their collective business as a team would grow nearly 50 percent over a 24-month period. Given this information, Laura and Donald were able to set aside the worries about splits and client access and sign off on a team agreement form.

Part of Laura's agreement with Donald, because of her larger asset base, was to become the team leader. They are now on pace for their projected growth. Their manager's role as a coach has become relatively easy as he uses Action Agreements to help keep them on track to develop constructive team habits while they build their 21st Century Financial Practice.

Planning and Assessing

As a team coach, you will want to help the team leader plan the first meeting. Begin the process of aligning the team around FastTrack Action Agreements 1 and 2 (described in Chapter 5), which takes them through developing their 5-year business plan and a metrics system that measures factors that will be indicators of their future success. Then work through

Agreements 3, 9 and 10, also described in Chapter 5. In the *Forming Stage*, you want everyone focused on analyzing where time is currently being wasted, and then clearly define and use that information to help delegate areas of responsibilities.

An important factor to consider in your efforts to coach a team through the *Forming* stage, is that each person is unique. Individual values differ, as do perceptions of important tasks and goals, and the individual differences will greatly influence a team's willingness and ability to make the necessary changes to build a successful 21st Century Financial Practice.

Those differences can be brought to the surface by assessing the *Team Building Style* and *General Employment Attitudes* of team members so that everyone can understand each other better. We have found two assessment tools that are especially useful for this stage of team development.

- **The Team Behavioral Style Assessment** – This tool is useful for all team members, as it describes a person's behavioral style in terms of "how you do what you do." Not "how well" you do it, but simply "how" you do it. Following the assessment, each team member receives a *Team Building Profile* which describes their Team Behavior Style in terms of four dimensions of normal behavior.

- **The General Employment Attitude Assessment** – This tool is useful for support personnel and specialists, especially when they join an existing team. The Attitudes Assessment indicates a person's *willingness to do* what is required plus his or her *willingness to change* in order to improve. Attitudes measure the clarity with which something is understood and valued. For example, if a person does not clearly understand what effective planning is all about, and does not place a high value on planning, he or she probably will not be willing to spend much time doing it. The *General Employment Report* that comes from this assessment focuses on qualities of empathy, practical thinking, system judgment, self-esteem, role awareness, and self-direction.

If you would like more information on these assessment tools, call 800-883-6582.

The *Forming Stage* shouldn't last long. Once the team members begin focusing on who's going to do what, the *Storming* will begin!

STAGE 2
STORMING

The Storming Stage is the most difficult stage to work through. Regardless of how well the Forming Stage is handled, conflict will begin to emerge as team members discover the following two realities of team life:

- Their responsibilities are more challenging than they had imagined.

- They must give up some of their independence in order to pursue team goals.

The welfare of each is bound in the welfare of all.

HELEN KELLER

When roles are not clearly defined, some team members may discover they are working harder than others and getting paid less. Much of the conflict over this may remain beneath the surface, expressed in cynical words and resistance, rather than angry outbursts. Other telltale signs might be members coming late to meetings or "forgetting" to complete tasks. Most people do not like conflict, so there is a tendency to deal with it by avoiding it as much as possible. High performance teams, Level 4 teams, cannot afford to do that.

It is vital to coach the team leader through this stage. Your coaching will enable him or her to emerge as the "real" team leader, not just the "designated" one, as you help the leader identify current areas of conflict and anticipate others that may emerge.

Steps to Resolve Conflict

1. Make certain that the facts are straight: who is doing what, when, where, or why. Never deal with conflict only on the basis of opinions and feelings.

2. Call a team meeting to address the conflict, following this format.

   A. Describe the facts of the situation. Ask the team member to confirm, correct, or add other facts. Stress that you only want "facts" for the purpose of describing what is happening. Keep working on the *description* until everyone agrees it is accurate.

   B. Ask team members for their thoughts on *why* the situation exists. Ask them to not evaluate each other's thoughts. Simply write them on a flip chart where everyone can see them. Once the entire list is completed, discuss them. Work on them until everyone agrees that the list is accurate.

   C. Ask team members for *solutions* that will eliminate items on the list of *why's* and resolve the conflict. Again, ask them to not evaluate each other's thoughts. Simply write the solutions on a flip chart where everyone can see them. Once the entire list is completed, discuss the solutions. Work on them until everyone agrees that they have one or more solutions that will resolve the conflict.

   D. Establish an *action plan* to implement the solution(s).

If passion drives you, let reason hold the reins.

Benjamin Franklin

The process of developing and implementing conflict resolution guidelines is important in order to progress on to the *Norming Stage*. Often the "aha" comes from discovering pockets of passive-aggressive resistance. Everything must be on the table during this stage; which involves revisiting all delegated areas of responsibility, coaching the group toward making the necessary adjustments, and agreeing upon an accountability process. The team conflict resolution process described above will accomplish that.

There is a tendency to try to ignore the *Storming Stage*, to avoid conflict at all costs. When that happens, teams can become stuck in this stage, lacking the means to move on. All high performing teams establish guidelines for conflict resolution. The guidelines above will help your teams resolve conflicts quickly, enabling them to keep focused on their goals.

The *Storming Stage* will last as long as the team members allow it to continue. A good team coach will help a team move quickly through this stage and on to the next. But this progression will not be without its setbacks.

"You've got to get up here ASAP!" shouted Joe over the phone. "Elliot isn't doing a f-n thing he said he was going to do and our support staff has gotten worse, not better – all because of Elliot."

Wow! Joe was the leader of a large and well-established team. Behind the outburst was the fact that Joe had assumed the role of team leader from Elliot, who was getting ready to retire. The team was composed of three financial advisors and three support personnel. Elliot was the founding father of the team, but all of the financial advisors were million-dollar producers in their own right. The support staff was a different story. They had been thrown together from available people.

I helped to set the stage for resolution through a teleconference that included their manager. Basically, Elliot's issue was that he did not want to officially retire. He liked coming into the office every day. But he didn't want to work very hard anymore (or at all, in Joe's opinion). Since the support staff didn't have much buy-in to the team goals, they picked up on this and played it for all it was worth.

The manager and I convinced Elliot to come up with a price and date for his buyout, by using the process described above. The team described the situation – discussed why it existed – explored solutions – and selected the solution that would best eliminate the "why it existed" and would best serve the team.

Two conference calls later the team was progressing on to the next stage, albeit with a different look. Elliot was no longer an official player with any true responsibilities.

The seriousness of this episode with Joe and Elliot should not be lost in the story. They came very close to a nasty divorce of a five million dollar business. Nobody would have been a winner if that had occurred. Their manager played a critical role in coaching the team toward a solution that assured fair treatment of Elliot while eliminating the conflict that his actions had created.

Stage 3
Norming

When you observe a consistent pattern of healthy interaction amongst team members, you are witnessing the emergence of group norms. At this point you will know that the team has reached the *Norming Stage*. It will be like "the pause that refreshes," and it will feel good.

These group norms start to develop when the team works together to create their 5-year business plan, metrics system and other action agreements in Stage 1. Redefining delegated areas of responsibility, developing an accountability process, and creating a set of team guidelines for resolving conflict in Stage 2, provides the framework and substance of those norms. Involving everyone in the development and implementation of the norms is what enables the team to reach the *Norming Stage*.

As mutual respect and trust emerge, you will coach the team toward a more meaningful exchange of facts, ideas, and opinions. The key to moving the team on to Stage 4 is working on problem solving and mutual accountability, all focused on one thing – continued improvement in attracting, servicing, and retaining affluent clients.

During this stage you will want to coach the team through Action Agreement 12 and help them develop their *Team Document Manual.* This simple binder that includes their business plan, metrics scorecards, delegated areas of responsibilities, and other helpful information, will become the single source for quick access to key policies and procedures that guide daily activity.

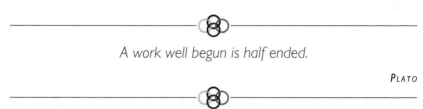

A work well begun is half ended.

PLATO

Because it feels so good to be a team at this point, the *Norming Stage* can evolve into a group comfort zone, if allowed to last – another "aha" for the team coach. Because everything is operating smoothly, communication is open, likability is strong, and people are doing their jobs; there is a tendency to become complacent. That is a red flag to you that this team needs to be urged to new heights.

This stage will continue as long as the team leader and coach allow it. You will often find teams stalling at this stage when one of two extremes are reached: the team leader is too detached and leaves everyone alone or the team leader is too involved and micro-manages the team.

As the team coach, you need to make certain that the team leader is truly leading the team into the *Performing Stage.* The team will need to be in a growth mode as they move into Stage 4, since that's where all the real achievements will take place.

STAGE 4
PERFORMING

In the Performing Stage, team interdependence emerges with all members contributing to successful decision making, meeting performance metrics, and solving problems directly related to the service of their clients. Everyone is willing to openly participate, perform beyond his or her delegated areas of responsibility, take personal ownership of team goals, and be accountable to each other. It doesn't get much better than this. It feels good to be a part of this team.

It will also feel good to coach a team at this stage through each remaining action agreement. As you continue to coach the team leader, you will also want to continue your check-ups with periodic visits to the weekly team meetings. Because of the high level of performance at this stage, your "aha's" are more likely to come from these meetings than from coaching the team leader.

Events are influenced by our very great desires.

WILLIAM JAMES

There is a tendency in the Performing Stage for the coach to assume that everything is fine, and it is to some extent. But life is a fluid process and so are teams, even teams who have reached the Performing Stage. One obstacle that can surface during this stage is that one team member might subtly become less of a contributor. If that happens, it will gradually begin to grind on the other team members and they will not want to ignore it. This is a delicate issue because the team is otherwise performing well and positive results are occurring. As the team coach, you will want to help the team leader to handle the matter in the following manner.

A. Gather all the facts from the team members. Both the behaviors involved and outcomes of that behavior need to be concisely documented. What is the individual in question doing or not doing, and what are the results?

B. Meet with the non-performing individual and present the situation, including the perceptions of other team members, supported by specifics. Make certain *not* to attack the individual. Merely focus on accountability for *doing* their job. The team coach should sit in on the meeting with the team leader and individual to show his or her support and provide a witness to what occurs.

C. Construct a written Action Agreement regarding the steps that will be taken by the non-performing individual.

D. Ask the non-performing individual to communicate the results of the meeting to the other team members. This should be part of the Action Agreement. This will strengthen team accountability.

E. The coach should then follow through with the team leader to support his or her efforts to bring the Action Agreement to completion.

When the non-performing individual is a senior team member, regardless of the team model, the entire team is at risk. The situation must be handled carefully, but firmly. In fact, the individual who has become less of a contributor could even be the team leader. In that case, you (the team coach) should assume the team leader's role for completing the above process.

12 MORE COMMANDMENTS OF SUCCESSFUL TEAMS

The completion of each *FastTrack Coaching Action Agreement* moves the team closer to the establishment of a successful 21st Century Financial Practice. Once a team is properly conceived, the following factors must be in place in order for the team to evolve into a successful Level 4 Team.

1. **Written business plan:** This goes beyond production numbers. Only 43 percent of the financial advisory teams in our latest survey had a long-range business plan. In fact, only 41 percent of surveyed financial planners reported having a written business plan for their own business. Don't make that mistake. Business plans draw the entire team toward one agreed-upon future state.

2. **Delegated areas of responsibility:** Simply assigning daily "urgent" tasks to assistants will block any possibility of building an effective team. Each team member needs clearly delegated areas of responsibility, all

focused on providing Ritz-Carlton service with FedEx efficiency. Ambiguity leads to inefficiency and confusion, and the team cannot afford either when dealing with affluent investors.

3. **Total integrity**: This should go without saying. The best business plan will blow up if there is any breach of integrity. Affluent clients want to know they can trust each team member, without exception.

4. **Solid work ethic**: This is a major gripe we encounter with established teams. In most cases, it stems from having skipped at least two of the first three commandments – particularly from failing to delegate areas of responsibility. Disparity in work ethic will ruin a team. Everyone must do his or her fair share.

5. **Effective team leadership**: No team will thrive without an effective leader. All of the research on teams, in every business setting, points to leadership as the most critical success factor. This is especially challenging with horizontal teams (a team of equals). Designate a leader – the right leader. It can be a revolving position, but every team needs definitive leadership.

6. **A single production number**: It is critical that everyone pull together and in the same direction. Having a single production number is a simple way to avoid conflict of interest. It's almost impossible to create the necessary team synergy while serving two masters (self and the team).

7. **Total accountability**: A well-defined plan is important; but without accountability for all parties involved, including the senior team member, the "plan" is rarely achieved. We have witnessed teams divorce over this issue alone.

8. **Team member shares**: Equity ownership plays a powerful role in fueling that important 110 percent commitment from every member of your team. Few things are as powerful as pride of ownership.

9. **Good communication**: Open, honest, and constructive communication will improve every aspect of your team. Weekly meetings, daily

huddles, and planning sessions can contribute to team growth. But if poorly planned and led, they can become a roadblock to team progress.

10.**Healthy growth**: As with any living organism, teams are either growing or dying. There is no in-between. Without growth, any synergy created will erode. Without that synergy, the ability to serve clients will soon be lost.

11.**Likability**: Team members don't need to be best friends, but they better respect each other and work hard to get along. Moodiness and jealousies will create unnecessary problems that can quickly bring a team to the point of no return.

12.**A formal team agreement**: A true wealth management practice needs a team agreement covering the basic future contingencies: death, dissolution of team, additional members, dispute resolution, etc. It can save both heartache and money.

In summary, developing a team requires the effort of every member of the team. How many people does it take to destroy a team? Only one. If that person is determined to undermine the team's efforts, is there anything anyone can do to turn that one person around? Not likely. Remember too that many teams fail for no other reason than that they were poorly conceived. And most importantly, as a FastTrack coach, you have a coaching contract with the entire team, but make certain that you personally coach the team leader. You begin your coaching of the team with the team leader and you end with the team leader. As he or she develops, so does the team.

Teams make a FastTrack coach's role more complex than when working with an individual financial advisor. But, even if creating and working according to Action Agreements may take more time, created with care they will guide teams just as effectively as they do individuals to work toward the creation of a 21st Century Financial Practice.

Team Self-Assessment

It's important to *never assume* that your team is as performance focused and operationally efficient as you would like to think. Exploring all the issues involved, and then rethinking the health of your team is a valuable exercise. The goal is to form a team in which everyone is pulling together to achieve a common 5-year business plan. The ideal is to have the *right people* with the *right attitudes* doing the *right activities*, the *right way*, for the *right reasons*.

The following tool is designed as a starting point for a quick team self-assessment. It will help you to analyze both attitudinal and behavioral factors. You will want to have every team member participate. When everyone has independently completed this assessment, use your findings as a basis for discussion.

Instructions

Direct each person to evaluate each of the following statements as things are now within the team — not how he or she would ideally like them to be. The more honest each person is with his or her answers, the greater the value will be derived. Each person should circle the number that best represents what he or she believes presently.

	Strongly Agree	Mildly Agree	Mildly Disagree	Strongly Disagree
1. Everyone has committed their career to the written long-range team business plan.	4	3	2	1
2. Everyone is accountable to the team for their delegated areas of responsibility.	4	3	2	1
3. Each team member is held to the same level of accountability.	4	3	2	1
4. All assets and production is pooled into one single team number.	4	3	2	1
5. Everyone subjugates their personal accomplishments to the accomplishments of the team.	4	3	2	1
6. Everyone has free access to all clients.	4	3	2	1

	STRONGLY AGREE	MILDLY AGREE	MILDLY DISAGREE	STRONGLY DISAGREE
7. Each team member works within the boundaries of a uniform team structure and established performance standards.	4	3	2	1
8. Everyone participates in decision making on team issues but acquiesces to the final decision of the team leader.	4	3	2	1
9. A team agreement, signed by all team members, spelling out every aspect of the long-term team working relationship, is in place.	4	3	2	1
10. Everyone has their individual goals linked to the written long-range team business plan.	4	3	2	1
11. All team members strive to facilitate open, honest, and productive communication within the team.	4	3	2	1
12. Everyone participates in structured weekly team meetings that are guided by objectives, follow an agenda, cover everyone's areas of responsibility, and concludes with action steps for each team member.	4	3	2	1
13. We praise in public, criticize in private, and always strive to build on individual strengths.	4	3	2	1
14. We personally train junior team members and support personnel.	4	3	2	1
15. Everyone honors all promises and commitments to the team.	4	3	2	1

After completing the above, add up all the circled numbers and record your total score on the following page.

Team Assessment – Scoring

My Score _____   **Maximum Score – 60**

Score

60 – 55 **You are doing a terrific job!** Continue pulling together, working toward your long-range business plan and refining your processes along the way.

54 – 45 **Good job.** You are doing many of the right things to develop a first class financial advisory team that is built to last. Pay attention to a few key areas and you will benefit tremendously.

44 – 34 **Average.** You are probably functioning more in the old sales and marketing model than you realize. Focus on turning your weaknesses into strengths and you will develop a first class financial advisory team.

< 34 **There is a lot of work to do.** You need to re-evaluate every aspect of your career; motivation, goals, commitment. etc.

You are very likely, almost guaranteed, to discover a range in the scores compiled by the individual members of a team. This is no cause for alarm; rather it's an opportunity to sit down and discuss these differences of opinion with the entire team. Keep in mind that no two people think alike; but as team coach, your objective is to uncover any hidden issues that might sabotage building a 21st Century Financial Practice.

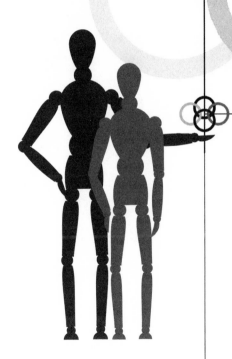

CHAPTER 11

BASIC TEAM STRUCTURES AND COMPENSATION AGREEMENTS

Personal satisfaction and happiness do seem to have a much greater importance for...top achievers than do material possessions.

GEORGE AND ALEC GALLUP

Money is not a problem until I believe it will solve my problems.

UNKNOWN

As a FastTrack coach, you are now entering the territory often described as a "slippery slope," because money is involved. Regardless of what people might say, the most critical issue regarding the structure of a team is individual remuneration. Which is the reason team structure and compensation agreements are not topics that get a coach's heart beating faster. However, the conflicts that typically arise in these areas will.

This is meat and potatoes stuff, presented in clear concise language that we have found to be helpful to individual financial advisors trying to make their wealth management team a success. Our objective is to provide a framework, a point of reference, for coaching a team through these critical and very personal issues. Heck, if there is serious disagreement over your suggestions, you have my permission to pass the blame back to us. Our ideas have been carefully formulated through the blood, sweat and tears of over 600 teams that we have personally coached.

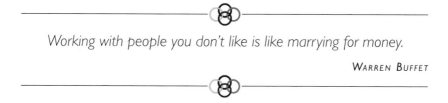

Working with people you don't like is like marrying for money.

WARREN BUFFET

TEAM STRUCTURE

We start with team structure, because once your structure is in place, you will have the foundation for creating a meaningful and fair compensation agreement. Following are four basic team structures you may encounter when coaching teams; as well as guidelines for team members to serve as a starting point for discussions.

VERTICAL TEAM – MODEL ONE

Senior team member, rookie junior team member, support personnel and specialist(s).

Within this model the senior team member remains in charge and controls the entire business. The composition of the team depends upon the corresponding growth and needs of the business, as determined by the senior team member. When a vertical team begins to experience success and it's evident that the current team members are contributing and working well together, it is not unusual for the senior team member to begin to relinquish control and team shares to valuable junior team members.

Senior team member

- Minimum length of service – 5 years.

- Minimum of $500 thousand production.

- Minimum of $60 million assets.

- Ability to *manage, lead* and *develop* others.

- Long-range team business plan in writing.

- Willingness to allow complete access to current clients by junior team member.

- One single production number.

- Willingness to develop a long-range compensation scale based on performance.

- Ability and willingness to be accountable to the team.

- Complete integrity.

Rookie junior team member

- Fully licensed.

- Meeting all firm guidelines for new team members.

- Exceptional work ethic.

- Willing to develop career as a team member joining a senior team member and forgo career as a single practitioner.

- Willing to use one single production number of the team.

- Ability to be accountable to team members, to be trained by senior team members, and earn team member shares through hard work and quality performance.

- Complete integrity.

- Ability to work well with senior team member, support personnel and specialists.

Support personnel

- Fully licensed.

- Possesses good people skills.

- Organized, able to multi-task and work well under pressure.

- Computer literate.

- Willing to be a full-time member of a team.

- Quality work ethic and complete integrity.

- Ability to manage all aspects of operational efficiency, including staffing issues.

- Ability to work well with clients.

- Ability to work well with senior and junior team members, and specialists.

Specialist(s): Tax, Marketing, Investments, Legal, and/or Insurance

- Fully licensed and certified within area of expertise.

- Good people skills.

- Willing to attach career to senior team member's business.

- Quality work ethic.

- High level of professionalism.

- Comfortable working with affluent investors.

- Complete integrity.

- Ability to work well with senior and junior team members, support personnel and other specialists.

Vertical Team – Model Two

Senior team member, experienced junior team member, support personnel and specialist(s).

Similar to Model One, this vertical model has the senior team member in charge of the entire business. The composition of the team depends upon the corresponding growth and needs of the business as determined by the senior team member.

Unlike Model One, the junior team member is experienced and has developed a personal book of business that is smaller than the senior team member's business. As this team experiences success, it is common for the senior team member to reward other team members with team shares in direct proportion to their performance.

Senior team member

- Minimum length of service – 5 years.

- Minimum of $500 thousand production.

- Minimum of $60 million assets.

- Ability to *manage, lead* and *work well* with others.

- Long-range team business plan in writing.

- Willingness to allow junior team member complete access to current clients.

- One single production number.

- Willingness to develop a long-range compensation scale based on performance.

- Ability to be accountable to the team.

- Complete integrity.

Experienced junior team member

- Smaller business (assets and production) than senior team member.

- Quality work ethic.

- Skills and expertise complementary to senior team member.

- Willingness to subjugate personal business to team business.

- Willingness to use one single production number of the team.

- Willingness to fully embrace long-range team business plan.

- Complete integrity.

- Ability to work well with senior team member, support personnel and specialists.

*It takes twenty years to build a reputation
and five minutes to ruin it.*

WARREN BUFFET

Support personnel

- Fully licensed.

- Possesses good people skills.

- Organized, able to multi-task and work well under pressure.

- Computer literate.

- Willing to be a full-time member of a team.

- Quality work ethic and complete integrity.

- Ability to manage all aspects of operational efficiency, including staffing issues.

- Ability to work well with clients.

- Ability to work well with senior and junior team members, and specialists.

Specialist(s): Tax, Marketing, Investments, Legal, and/or Insurance

- Fully licensed and certified within area of expertise.

- Good people skills.

- Willing to attach career to senior team member's business.

- Quality work ethic.

- High level of professionalism.

- Comfortable working with affluent investors.

- Complete integrity.

- Ability to work well with senior and junior team members, support personnel and other specialists.

VERTICAL TEAM – MODEL THREE
Senior team member, support personnel and/or specialist(s).

Within this vertical model, the senior team member is the only official financial advisor on the team. The number of support persons and specialists will be determined by the scope and growth of the senior team member's business.

It is not unusual for one support person to be a CFP and be responsible for the financial planning for clients, while another might serve a more operational role, and a specialist might provide clients with all estate and insurance issues.

Similar to the other vertical models, when the team starts to experience success and the support personnel and specialist(s) become indispensable, team shares should be awarded according to performance and value.

Senior team member

- Minimum length of service – 5 years.

- Minimum of $500 thousand production.

- Minimum of $60 million assets.

- Ability to *manage, lead* and *work well* with others.

- Long-range team business plan in writing.

- Willingness to allow support personnel complete access to current clients and financial matters.

- One single production number.

- Willingness to develop a long-range compensation scale based on performance.

- Ability to be accountable to the support personnel as true team members.

- Complete integrity.

Support personnel

- Fully licensed.

- Possesses good people skills.

- Organized, able to multi-task and work well under pressure.

- Computer literate.

- Willing to be a full-time member of a team.

- Quality work ethic and complete integrity.

- Ability to manage all aspects of operational efficiency, including staffing issues.

- Ability to work well with clients.

- Ability to work well with senior team member and specialists.

Specialist(s): Tax, Marketing, Investments, Legal, and/or Insurance

- Fully licensed and certified within area of expertise.

- Good people skills.

- Willing to attach career to senior team member's business.

- Quality work ethic.

- High level of professionalism.

- Comfortable working with affluent investors.

- Complete integrity.

- Ability to work well with senior team member, support personnel and other specialists.

HORIZONTAL TEAM – MODEL FOUR

Senior team members, support personnel, specialist(s) and/or junior team member (rookie or experienced).

This is a model of equals. Two senior team members decide to merge their respective businesses as equals with equal compensation. The defining characteristics are similar levels of production and assets. Age and length of service are not critical in the formation of a functional horizontal team.

After a period of team success when a discrepancy in age exists, it is not unusual for the senior (in age) to begin thinking in terms of working less, semi-retirement, or even full retirement. This requires a redistribution of compensation and a corresponding restructuring of individual areas of responsibility.

Senior team members

- Minimum length of service – 5 years.

- Minimum of $500 thousand production.

- Minimum of $60 million assets.

- Willingness to pool all assets and production into a single team number.

- Ability to appoint and support one senior team member as *team leader*.

- Long-range team business plan in writing.

- Complete integrity.

- Quality work ethic.

- Complementary skills, knowledge, and expertise.

- Willingness to be cross-functional with other senior team member when necessary.

- Ability to agree on compensation and bonus for support personnel.

- Ability to be accountable to other senior team member and the other team members.

Support personnel

- Fully licensed.

- Possesses good people skills.

- Organized, able to multi-task and work well under pressure.

- Computer literate.

- Willing to be a full-time member of a team.

- Quality work ethic and complete integrity.

- Ability to manage all aspects of operational efficiency, including staffing issues.

- Ability to work well with clients.

- Ability to work well with senior team members, junior team members and specialists.

Specialist(s): Tax, Marketing, Investments, Legal, and/or Insurance

- Fully licensed and certified within area of expertise.

- Good people skills.

- Willing to attach career to senior team member's business.

- Quality work ethic.

- High level of professionalism.

- Comfortable working with affluent investors.

- Complete integrity.

- Ability to work well with senior and junior team members and support personnel.

Junior team member (rookie and/or experienced)

(See guidelines for Vertical Team – Models One and Two)

TEAM COMPENSATION GUIDELINES

Team compensation should be addressed during the *Forming Stage* of team development for all vertical and horizontal teams. Team members must perceive compensation allocation as performance-driven and fair. Ignoring this issue or assuming everything is okay without clarification will lead to unanswered questions that frequently have a negative impact on team performance.

Following are seven key principles that should guide your approach to coaching teams on issues relating to compensation.

1. The team should develop their 5-year business plan and metrics system first so they are clear about where they want to go, how they plan to get there, and what the projected incremental increases in assets, production, and recurring revenue will be.

2. In Vertical Team Models One and Two – The team compensation split for the first year should be based on each senior and junior financial advisor's percentage of their previous year's combined production. Beginning the second year, the split should be based on each advisor's projected contribution to the next year's business growth. As you will discover, this differs slightly in each of the vertical teams.

3. When a junior financial advisor's efforts contribute to the *growth* of assets and achieving business metrics, he or she should be rewarded with a corresponding incremental growth in compensation percentage. This should continue until the junior financial advisor's percentage achieves parity with the senior financial advisor, as long as his or her contribution to business growth also continues. Senior financial advisors (senior team members) who resist this incremental percentage increase should be persuaded that this is vital for two reasons: 1) To provide the proper incentive to achieve the metrics established and 2) To prevent the loss of good people.

4. In Vertical Team Models One and Two – Compensation for support personnel should be absorbed by the senior financial advisor (senior team member) during the first year. Beginning the second year, compensation should be allocated among all advisors on the basis of their compensation split percentages.

5. Support personnel compensation can be in the form of salary, percentage shares, and bonuses. Increases should be a reward for performance and performance improvement. Some suggested criteria are listed below.

   • Subjective – attitude, teamwork, client feedback, and initiative.

- Quantitative – quarterly goals for their role, client contact goals, continued professional education, specific projects or focuses for each quarter.

6. When two or more senior financial advisors are considering the formation of a horizontal team, factors beyond trailing 12-month production numbers need to be factored into the initial percentage split. If the initial percentage split is not 50/50, achieving parity should be a short-term objective.

7. As teams build their business by successfully attracting affluent clients and increasing recurring revenue, they will need and want to increase their support personnel staff, particularly specialists in areas like financial planning and taxes. At that point, the percentage of total production allocated to support personnel also needs to be increased. The financial advisors should continue to share that allocation on the basis of their compensation split.

Following are examples of how these principles can be applied in each of the four team models. The growth percentages are kept simple to make the examples themselves as simple as possible.

EXAMPLE 1
VERTICAL TEAM – MODEL ONE

Senior financial advisor, junior financial advisor (rookie) and support personnel.

Objective: Their 5-year business plan and metrics lead them to project consistent team growth of 15 percent per year. Both advisors want to work hard and grow the business. With some apprehension, the senior advisor agrees to achieve compensation parity in six years at an increase of 7.5 percent per year. They also agree to increase support personnel compensation .5 percent per year, up to a maximum of 5 percent. The senior financial advisor will assume full support in the first year, and the junior financial advisor will begin sharing that expense in the second year, using the current year's team percentage split. Everything, of course, is predicated on maintaining a 15 percent annual growth rate.

Previous Year

- Senior financial advisor – $750 thousand production, $90 million assets, 55 percent recurring revenue.

- Junior financial advisor – $135 thousand production, $12 million assets, 90 percent recurring revenue.

- Support personnel – received one percent of senior financial advisor's production.

The first year compensation split will be based on each advisor's percentage of the previous year's combined production of $885,000. The senior financial advisor will receive 85 percent; the junior financial advisor, 15 percent. For the first year, the support personnel compensation will continue to come from the senior financial advisor's production.

First Year – Production increase of 15 percent to $1,017,750.

- Senior financial advisor – $865,087.50 (85 percent).

- Junior financial advisor – $152,662.50 (15 percent).

- Support personnel – $10,177.50 (one percent, which comes from the senior advisor's compensation).

Per the agreement made when the team organized, the junior financial advisor's team share starting in the second year will increase 7.5 percent per year so long as the annual team growth is 15 percent or more. The junior financial advisor will also begin to share the compensation expense of support personnel, using the current team percentage split.

Second Year – Production increase of 15 percent to $1,170,412.50.

- Senior financial advisor – $907,069.69 (77.5 percent).

- Junior financial advisor – $263,342.81 (22.5 percent).

- Support personnel – $17,556.19 (1.5 percent – which comes from both advisors' compensation using the current compensation split of 77.5 percent from the senior financial advisor and 22.5 percent from the junior financial advisor).

Production increases 15 percent each year, and the junior financial advisor receives a 7.5 percent increase in compensation share each year. Support personnel also receive a .5 percent increase each year.

Third Year – Production increase of 15 percent to $1,345,974.38.

- Senior financial advisor – $942,182.07 (70 percent).

- Junior financial advisor – $403,792.31 (30 percent).

- Support personnel – $26,919.49 (2 percent – split 70/30).

Fourth Year – Production increase of 15 percent to $1,547,870.54.

- Senior financial advisor – $967,419.09 (62.5 percent).

- Junior financial advisor – $580,451.45 (37.5 percent).

- Support personnel – $38,696.76 (2.5 percent – split 62.5/37.5).

The team will probably begin adding new support personnel at this point – and may actually increase the percentage allocated to those positions. They would probably agree to continue the percent each advisor allocates.

Fifth Year – Production increase of 15 percent to $1,780,051.12.

- Senior financial advisor – $979,028.12 (55 percent).

- Junior financial advisor – $801,023.00 (45 percent).

- Support personnel – $53,401.53 (3 percent – split 55/45).

Sixth Year – Production increase of 15 percent to $2,047,058.79.

- Senior financial advisor – $1,023,529.40 (50 percent).

- Junior financial advisor – $1,023,529.39 (50 percent).

- Support Personnel – $102,352.94 (5 percent – split 50/50).

Because they maintained the projected 15 percent annual increase in production, the senior and junior financial advisors achieve parity by the end of the fifth year. They now split the compensation and expenses, including support personnel compensation, 50/50.

Example 2
Vertical Team – Model Two

Senior financial advisor, junior financial advisor (experienced) and support personnel.

Objective: Their 5-year business plan and metrics lead them to project consistent team growth of 12 percent per year, a lower rate than the team in Example 1, for the following reasons. The senior financial advisor wants to work hard and grow the business. The junior financial advisor recruited to the team has, for whatever reasons, reached a plateau. However, he does bring assets and special skills and is capable of servicing affluent clients effectively. The advantage to the junior financial advisor is that his income will grow even though his allocation will remain the same at 25 percent. Support personnel and other team expenses are projected to increase .5 percent to 1 percent annually, up to 5 percent maximum. Beginning with the second year, the junior financial advisor will also cover 25 percent of support personnel expenses.

This is a deviation from the principles stated above, but with valid reasons.

Previous Year

- Senior financial advisor – $750 thousand production, $90 million assets, 55 percent recurring revenue.

- Junior financial advisor – $250 thousand production, $35 million assets, 60 percent recurring revenue.

- Support personnel – received one percent of senior financial advisor's production.

Per agreement, the compensation split will be based on each advisor's percentage of the previous year's combined production of $1,000,000. The senior financial advisor will receive 75 percent and the junior financial advisor 25 percent. For the first year, the support personnel compensation will come from the senior financial advisor's production.

First Year – Production increases 12 percent to $1,120,000.

- Senior financial advisor – $840,000 (75 percent).

- Junior financial advisor – $280,000 (25 percent).

- Support personnel – $11,200 (1 percent of the total compensation, shared 75/25).

Second Year – Production increases 12 percent to $1,254,400.

- Senior financial advisor – $940,800 (75 percent).

- Junior financial advisor – $313,600 (25 percent).

- Support personnel – $18,816 (1.5 percent of total production which is shared 75/25).

Third Year – Production increases 12 percent to $1,404,928.

- Senior financial advisor – $1,053,696 (75 percent).

- Junior financial advisor – $351,232 (25 percent).

- Support personnel – $28,098.56 (2 percent of total production which is shared 75/25).

Example 3
Vertical Team – Model Three

Senior financial advisor and support personnel.

Objective: Their 5-year business plan and metrics lead them to project 15 percent annual growth. The senior financial advisor and support personnel are all motivated to work hard and grow the business. Rather than team with another financial advisor, this individual prefers to delegate responsibilities and develop support personnel to function as team specialists, e.g., *Certified Financial Planner, Practice Manager,* etc. – and plans to allocate up to 10 percent of the team's production to support personnel compensation.

The advantage to the senior financial advisor is being able to retain a much larger portion of the business while developing a team of support personnel who can specialize in areas that will help attract, service, and retain affluent investors.

The advantage to the support personnel is increased income potential while contributing as a specialist in a wealth management team. A second specialist will be added the second year. Once again, 15 percent annual growth is the critical component for projecting compensation.

Previous Year

- Senior financial advisor – $750 thousand production, $90 million assets, 55 percent recurring revenue.

- Support personnel – currently receiving 1 percent of the senior financial advisor's production.

First Year: Production increase of 15 percent to $862,500.

- Senior financial advisor – $849,562 (98.5 percent).

- Support personnel – $12,938 (1.5 percent).

The senior financial advisor begins with a 1.5 percent allocation to support personnel – and plans to increase that amount, as needed each year. That "need" is based on having the support to successfully achieve the 15 percent annual growth in production.

Second Year – Production increase of 15 percent to $905,625.

- Senior financial advisor – $869,400 (96 percent).

- Support personnel "A" and "B" – $36,225 (4 percent).

To continue a 15 percent growth rate, an additional support person was added to the team.

Third Year – Production increase of 15 percent to $1,041,468.75.

- Senior financial advisor – $978,980 (94 percent).

- Support personnel "A" and "B" – $62,488 (6 percent).

Fourth Year – Production increase of 15 percent to $1,197,689.06.

- Senior financial advisor – $1,101,873 (92 percent).

- Support personnel "A" and "B" – $95,816 (8 percent).

Fifth Year – Production increases 15 percent to $1,377,342.42.

- Senior financial advisor – $1,239,608 (90 percent).

- Support personnel "A" and "B" – $137,734 (10 percent).

The financial advisor can work toward parity between support personnel at any time between the second and sixth years. Although percentages will not change, bonuses can be used to stimulate productivity and growth.

EXAMPLE 4
HORIZONTAL TEAM – MODEL 4

Senior financial advisor "A", senior financial advisor "B", support personnel "A" and support personnel "B".

Objective: Their 5-year business plan and metrics lead them to project consistent team growth of 15 percent per year, and both senior financial advisors are committed to working hard to grow the business. Compensation parity is an important factor. They should either begin at 50/50 or set a goal to accomplish it within two or three years (rather than five to six years as the team in Example 1). This will depend on the level and quality of business each senior financial advisor initially brings to the team. They should assess their respective businesses with special attention paid to production, assets, revenue producing assets, recurring revenue, ideal and potential households, and their past three-year business trend. They also agree that up to 5 percent will be allocated to support personnel, divided equally starting at 2 percent of production (1 percent each).

PREVIOUS YEAR	ADVISOR "A"	ADVISOR "B"
Production	$1.2 million	$800 thousand
Assets	$150 million	$90 million
Revenue producing assets	$110 million	$80 million
Recurring revenue	40 percent	80 percent
Potential and ideal households	165	145
3-year business trend	< 20 percent from $1.5 million	> 50 percent from $400,000

If applying the typical split of the production totals, financial advisor "A" would be allocated 60 percent and financial advisor "B" 40 percent of the combined production. In this case there are reasons to adjust that. Senior financial advisor "B" has strengths that must be considered as well as 80 percent of recurring revenue and a 3-year trend of +50 percent. In contrast, senior financial advisor "A" has 40 percent recurring revenue and a -20 percent 3-year business trend. They agreed to a 55/45 split the first year, and then parity beginning with the second year. It tends to be simplest when support personnel share from the overall team production numbers, 2 percent of $2,300,000, which is $46,000, as shown in the example for the first year.

The issue of compensation split must be agreed upon by all parties and needs to take in more variables than production. Both parties must view the compensation split as fair.

First Year – Production increase of 15 percent to $2,300,000:

- Senior financial advisor "A" – $1,265,000 (55 percent)

- Senior financial advisor "B" – $1,035,000 (45 percent)

- Support personnel "A" and "B" – $46,000 (2 percent)

Second Year – Production increase of 15 percent to $2,645,000:

- Senior financial advisor "A" – $1,322,500 (50 percent)

- Senior financial advisor "B" – $1,322,500 (50 percent)

- Support personnel "A" and "B" – $79,350 (3 percent)

Third Year – Production increase of 15 percent to $3,04,750:

- Senior financial advisor "A" – $1,520,875 (50 percent)

- Senior financial advisor "B" – $1,520,875 (50 percent)

- Support personnel "A" and "B" – $121,670 (4 percent)

In the old transactional model of Wall Street, financial advisor "A" would have insisted on always maintaining a larger percentage based on the initial production figures. But in the old model, there was not always the need for a collaborative effort in order to reach higher production targets. The junior broker did the grunt work, whether it was cold calling, licking stamps, organizing seminars, or handling the small accounts.

In today's world the synergism required to effectively deliver solutions for the multidimensional aspects of an affluent client's personal finances requires a true synergy amongst all team members. Not only must everyone pull together, everyone must also have clearly delegated areas of responsibility that will be attended to in order for the team to experience the growth outlined in their 5-year business plan.

During the first three years following the formation of their team (Vertical Team – Model One: Senior, two juniors, and two support personnel), everyone made more money. Business was up, the stock market was hitting new highs, and the junior financial advisors earned additional team shares while the support staff received generous bonuses. All was well.

Two years later, on the heels of one of the most challenging markets, growth has been extremely difficult and achieved only by developing new affluent relationships. A problem arose when the senior financial advisor woke-up one morning with a visceral feeling that Mark, one of the junior partners, was not doing his share of new business development.

Acting rather impulsively, the senior financial advisor marched into his manager's office, stated his case, and explained why he wanted the manager to intercede and develop a formula that would cut Mark's compensation – dramatically.

Fortunately his manager talked the senior financial advisor out of doing anything before thoroughly reviewing his team's metrics and determining who had done what; and then called me. His fear was that a successful 5-year team could blow-up if this incidence was mishandled.

Three conference calls later (first with the manager, then the senior team member, and finally with the entire team) all team members were outside their respective comfort zones. Rather than targeting all angst against Mark, it was quickly determined that there was plenty of blame to go around. Nobody, other than the senior advisor, had been bringing in new business.

Fortunately I can tell you that currently everyone is accountable to specific fixed daily activities that require out of the office face time with centers-of-influence or qualified prospects. Instead of reworking compensation splits, their manager has permission from the team to hold each individual accountable for doing his or her fixed daily activities.

Is there a happy ending? Not yet. It's a work in progress, but at least they are all doing the necessary activities to bring in new business; and compensation is now linked to individual new business development along with the gross production of the team. FastTrack coaching a team is serious business that can be fraught with land mines, often revolving around team structure and compensation.

All of this is a prelude to the song itself which must be learned.

PLATO

The 21st Century Financial Practice team is made up of knowledge workers and solutions providers and it is important that everyone is able to look ahead toward a better future. Building a compensation package that meets everyone's needs requires accountability for each individual's contributions and it must have a performance flexibility component built in so that when business is off, team members will not get a raise. Such compensation arrangements are imperative when building a team to last. A growing functional team should never be arguing over money.

ACHIEVER
GROUP
COACHING

CHAPTER 12

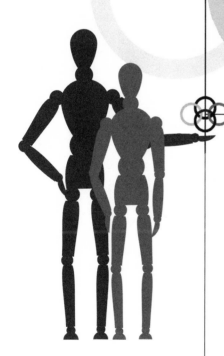

THE ACHIEVER GROUP
COACHING CONCEPT

Fall seven times, stand up eight.
JAPANESE PROVERB

Of all the things I've done, the most vital is coordinating the talents of those who work for us, and pointing them toward a certain goal.
WALT DISNEY

Each chapter to this point has focused on using FastTrack Coaching to accelerate the development of individual financial professionals or wealth management teams seeking to target affluent investors. You may be asking, "Can the FastTrack Coaching approach be applied in other situations as well? If so, does it have to be done on an individual basis, or can a group coaching approach be used?" The answer to both questions is "absolutely yes."

What we describe here is a unique form of coaching – group coaching. We call it *Achiever Group Coaching*. Those who participate share a common bond – the need to effectively perform at a higher level than they are presently. It's unique because as the group members progress toward reaching their goals, coaching becomes a shared task. The person assigned to coach the group becomes a coach-facilitator as the group members evolve into a participant-coach role. It's a powerful process and has some very interesting roots.

In 1935, a New York stockbroker named Bill Wilson worked together with Robert Holbrook-Smith, a doctor from Akron, Ohio, to overcome their common drinking problem. What they developed is known today as Alcoholics Anonymous, a worldwide fellowship of 2 million men and women who "share their experience, strength and hope with each other that they may solve their common problem and help others to recover from alcoholism."

Over 500,000 similar self-help groups flourish today for people with a wide range of compulsions and addictions. The principle guiding them is simple: people who share a common problem come together and discover that they have something positive to offer one another. That "something" ranges from emotional support to friendship to specific expertise. It's a bond that provides the healing and pulls them through. The sponsoring organization simply creates the atmosphere and provides a structured process.

Achiever Groups do not have the same purpose as self-help groups, but they do have some similarities. Rather than a group of people meeting to support each other in their quest to break a specific habit, Achiever Groups pull professionals of similar stature and circumstance together to support one another, as they strive to improve individual performance. Because these people know that they must improve their performance, and do it quickly, they too benefit from the emotional support, friendship, and expertise of others who share the same need to venture outside their comfort zone and grow.

It matters not what you call them – self-help, mutual aid, support systems – they are the fastest growing component of the human service industry. Nor is it surprising. Man is a social animal who throughout his history has banded together for problem solving and survival...

H. W. Demone

The group dynamics, which make it possible for the members to grow, evolve out of several group processes that are designed to help the group members solve common problems that are blocking them from higher levels of performance. When facilitated by a skilled coach, these processes provide the fuel for accelerated achievement.

One of the obstacles to success lurking below the surface in the financial services business sector is the "Lone-Ranger" character of some financial advisors, who are also suspicious of their comrades. On numerous occasions, I have had financial advisors ask me to evaluate their new marketing materials, with a very strict request for confidentiality. What makes this so humorous is that the materials I'm reviewing were developed from templates that I provided. And, since everyone in their office has the same templates, they would gain much more by helping each other than by being so secretive. At times you too may encounter financial advisors who harbor an almost phobic distrust that has no basis. If those advisors participate in an Achiever Group, they will learn to overcome their distrust.

PROCESSES THAT MAKE AN ACHIEVER GROUP SUCCESSFUL

You will appreciate the power and possibilities of Achiever Groups as you read the following brief descriptions of six group processes that contribute significantly to their success. Particularly note the role of the coach-facilitator in each process.

1. **Group cohesion** – A collection of individuals will emerge as a cohesive group if and when they truly experience being accepted as they are. In order for that to happen, they must be able to share thoughts and feelings without criticism.

   The coach-facilitator sets the example and the others will follow. Work hard to accept everyone; even those you suspect may be inclined to be negative or disruptive. The idea is to let the ground rules be everyone's code of conduct guide and let the participants, as much as possible, hold each other accountable to act accordingly. Use words of encouragement rather than criticism. Allow anyone to say anything at any time. Urge them to leave the negatives behind and move ahead. I have witnessed many an attitude transformation through the Achiever Group process.

2. **Individual goals and fixed daily activities** – The purpose of an Achiever Group is to use peer support and pressure to activate each participant's Achievement Cycle (See Chapter 8). During the first meeting for the group, every participant is required to commit to a serious goal referred to as a "Quantum Growth Commitment." Next, they each define specific fixed daily activities that must be done in order to achieve their lofty goals. This commitment is made public and discussed by the entire group. The following probing questions will be asked. Is this goal realistic? Is it challenging enough? Are the fixed daily activities doable?

Each participant will be pulled outside his or her comfort zone from this point forward.

At the onset of establishing Quantum Growth Commitments and fixed daily activities, accountability becomes the thread that is woven throughout the fabric of these meetings. As a coach-facilitator, your role is to make certain that each individual is held accountable for the fixed daily activities they have defined. Doing those activities will ensure that the Achievement Cycle remains activated for each participant.

3. **Modeling** – Achiever Groups typically meet six times for 45 to 90 minutes, at two-week intervals. During the meetings, numerous topics relating to achievement will be covered, but the constant will always be individual accountability updates. During the updates, the coach-facilitator should encourage individuals to share success stories with the group. The stories will typically follow a pattern: stating a problem followed by how they coped with or solved the problem.

Stories are important because they provide models that give the others hope and encouragement as well as specific strategies to try. Of course not all participants will have a success story, but one or two usually will, and that's all you need. The issue for you as coach-facilitator is to make certain that everyone is modeling the behavior and attitudes of a high-achiever, which is why being engaged in their Achievement Cycle is the critical issue.

Although success stories naturally occur, you will find that you may need to encourage this form of sharing. Believe it or not, in this forum people tend to resist telling their good news or bragging. Your role is to facilitate the discussion with a well-directed question such as, "Can any of you think of a situation where you encountered and overcame this kind of problem?" Talk about the use of stories early in the group experience, and explain the importance of keeping them focused and short. Even then, you may find it necessary to stop some stories from turning into long-winded "war stories."

4. **The helper role** – It goes without saying that everyone in the group needs help with improving their performance. After all, that's the reason they are there. But the most critical help given will be from each other and for each other. When a group works to help one another, it is often the person in the helper role that benefits the most. Concern begins to shift from their personal problems to another's problems; consequently their energy is directed toward helping the other person find and sustain a solution that works. In the Achiever Group setting, that process is formalized by pairing group members into Working Partner relationships.

   As coach-facilitator, you will want to be alert to helper role opportunities and do everything you can to encourage group members to step into that role. In fact, as often as possible, avoid stepping into that role yourself, unless it's the only option.

5. **Brainstorming** – Brainstorming has become such a familiar process that it's easy to forget how it should work and overlook its benefits. The purpose of brainstorming is to get rid of blinders and explore a variety of possible solutions or ideas. It's a prerequisite to breaking out of one's comfort zone. However, group members must be able to voice those solutions and ideas knowing that no one will criticize them in any way. In fact, participants in a brainstorming process must be encouraged to express any idea that comes to mind, regardless of how crazy the idea may seem. The goal is quantity of ideas and solutions, not quality.

   The coach-facilitator will need to explain the purpose of brainstorming and make certain that the ground rules are clear. If the group deviates from the rules in any way, stop the process, remind them again of how it should be done, and then continue. The challenge for the group is to build from the ideas of others.

6. **The Achievement Cycle** – Becoming a member of an Achiever Group will not necessarily assure participants of success. But, understanding and living the Achievement Cycle will. The cycle involves thinking, feel-

ing, and doing – but must be cycled in the proper sequence. A person cannot think his or her way to success; and certainly can't feel the way to success. Instead, what a person does is what really matters and brings about success. I realize that I risk appearing redundant by emphasizing this sixth step, but this cycle is the context within which every aspect of achievement evolves. You will want your Achiever Group members living and breathing the Achievement Cycle – and possibly even teaching it to their spouses, children and friends!

...it does not need sociologists, psychiatrists, historians or priests to draw our attention to the simple fact that people who share a certain problem might possibly have something to offer each other. That 'something' might be emotional support, material aid, friendship, technical expertise, or a refuge from discrimination, hatred, stigma or quite simply 'the world out there'.

DAVID ROBINSON AND STUART HENRY

As I indicated earlier, the emphasis on doing is introduced in your first Achiever Group meeting. The Achievement Cycle will be explained and actually experienced by the participants in the second meeting, and will continue to be the driving force behind everything they do from that point on. If you haven't already figured it out, the most important of these six processes is the Achievement Cycle.

WHO SHOULD PARTICIPATE IN AN ACHIEVER GROUP?

Participants can come from almost anywhere in your organization. The common thread in each group must be the need to improve performance in a defined area. In fact, it's not uncommon to have people assigned to a group with a specific mandate from their manager.

Homogeneous groups do work best. Those would be groups made up of people that do the same type of work or occupy similar positions, although their specific areas needing improvement could differ. Following are some possible groups that may be formed.

- Financial advisors who are interested in improving their business.

- Managers who need to learn how to coach.

- Operations and support people who need to become more efficient in specific areas.

- Technical people who need to manage projects more effectively.

- Junior advisors or rookie junior advisors who need to accelerate their learning and growth.

- Team leaders who want to take their teams to higher levels.

Groups made up of people from different work areas and levels of the organization can also work, but the lateral task differences and vertical hierarchy differences will be more pronounced, which almost always makes it more difficult for group cohesion to occur.

In the Achiever Group setting, the stage is set for all players to act out the achiever role assigned to them, focused on improving their performance in a well-defined area. In time, they will take on the new roles indicated above – model, working partner and coach. Then, when they leave the group, they will take those roles with them, ready to step into them when new situations arise. That is one great side benefit of the Achiever Group experience.

In Chapter 13 we will look more closely at specific coach-facilitator actions that will help to produce high achievement among members of your Achiever Groups.

CHAPTER 13

FACILITATING AN ACHIEVER GROUP MEETING

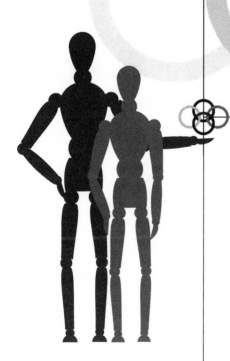

It's kinda fun to do the impossible.
WALT DISNEY

Learning does not occur because behavior has been primed (stimulated); it occurs because behavior, primed or not, is reinforced.
B. F. SKINNER

In Chapter 1, we defined FastTrack Coaching as a collaborative process between coach and financial professional, designed to focus and accelerate personal and professional development. Has our combining the terms *coach* and *facilitator* confused you? If so, our reasoning is that both are taking place. You coach people, but you facilitate the meeting. Coaching is something you do to people. Facilitation is something you do with people.

As coach-facilitator you will lead the meetings, but your primary role will be to facilitate discussion as you work to bring out the contributions of each group member. You will be looking for ways to build group cohesion and implement modeling; to focus on goals and doing fixed activities; and advance the helper role, brainstorming, and achievement cycle processes discussed in Chapter 13.

Establishing Quantum Growth Commitments with corresponding fixed daily activities, even though it is an out-of-comfort zone experience for the group members, will be a basic component of your initial meeting. The accountability updates during subsequent sessions will often require delicate handling, as illustrated in Kerry's story.

"I wanted to go first because I'm here to tell you how embarrassed I am about my sorry state of affairs. It's been so long since I've committed to any serious goals that I didn't have a clue about what I was capable of doing on a daily basis," confessed Kerry to his peers. He concluded his accountability update with, "I've allowed myself to simply do rookie activities, which is ridiculous! I'm a 17-year veteran with a large book of business. With the permission of the group, I will remain committed to my goal, but I've got to change all of my fixed daily activities."

The Quantum Growth Commitment goal Kerry set in his first meeting had not matched the fixed daily activities he had defined. After two weeks of dabbling in those "rookie activities" as he called them, Kerry realized that it was time to step up and be accountable for that — first to himself and then to the group. Through the coach-facilitator's delicate handling, following Kerry's confessional, all the group members found themselves looking more closely at and then adjusting their own lists of fixed daily activities.

Kerry was the unofficial leader of this group of financial advisors. Not only was he the largest producer, he was also the assistant manager and had a very strong personality. If Kerry said something was okay, the rest of the group was comfortable with whatever it might be. Consequently after Kerry's update, everyone in the group adapted their fixed daily activities to mirror what Kerry had committed to doing. If he was going to block a certain amount of time for cold calling, so were they.

That's why Kerry had asked for permission to give his accountability update first during that second session. He knew that he set the standard, and realized that everyone needed to be given permission to be honest and change their fixed daily activities if they were going to ever achieve their Quantum Growth Commitments.

In small groups, students are more likely to explore possibilities, ask questions, take risks, and learn from their mistakes.

BARBARA GLESNER FINES

It worked out beautifully, and led to other group members sharing their success stories at subsequent meetings. But it did require a bit of delicate finessing by the coach-facilitator, yours truly, during that second session.

Although you will be setting the agenda, you need to be willing to make adjustments to meet the needs of the group, as you pay close attention to how people in the meeting are working together and progressing toward their individual and collective goals. Some techniques you will want to use are listed below.

- Raise questions to challenge thinking and bring out different viewpoints.

- Help the group create lists of important points.

- Restate or summarize the issues as appropriate.

- Facilitate the accountability that enables participants to remain true to the Achievement Cycle by doing what they committed to do.

- Provide handouts and use other presentation media to clarify main points.

- Share your own ideas when appropriate, usually after everyone else has expressed theirs.

When facilitating your meetings, you also need to be aware of simple non-verbal cues that define the tone of the meeting. In fact, even where you sit with respect to the group matters. If you are in front, with everyone facing you, everyone's attention will be on you. Instead, arrange everyone, including you, at a round or U-shaped table so there is good eye contact between all group members.

KEY PROCESSES

There are six key processes that you will need to facilitate at various points during the six Achiever Group meetings. Following are brief explanations and guidelines for each.

1. **Establish ground rules** (First meeting):

Because of the dynamics and processes that define the Achiever Group coaching concept, it's important to establish a set of *ground rules* at the beginning of the first meeting. Ground rules serve three functions for you as coach-facilitator.

- Ground rules guide your behavior as much as they do the behavior of the group. You cannot expect the group members to do what you are not willing to do yourself. Everyone then knows what to expect and what will be expected of them.

- Ground rules provide you with a teaching tool for establishing group norms. Rule number two says, "Attend every session, and don't let anything keep you from doing so." That sounds simple, but it won't be. You will hear all the typical excuses why someone cannot attend a meeting, and you will need to teach them ways to put everything else aside and be there, for their own good and the good of the group. Obviously, you will need to be flexible with emergencies.

- Ground rules serve as a diagnostic tool to help you pinpoint negative attitudes and disruptive behavior. If that happens, present it to the group as a problem and have them work out a solution that is acceptable to every group member.

GROUND RULES

A. Make a commitment to learn and grow through the Achiever Group process.

B. Attend every session, and don't let anything keep you from doing so.

C. Be accountable to the group, and allow others to be accountable to you.

D. Perform every exercise and assignment even when you're not yet convinced of its value.

E. Bring a big heart, an open mind, and a positive attitude to every session.

F. Arrive at each session ready to have fun!

It should be made clear that these ground rules are not optional. They are givens, and their acceptance must be a condition for Achiever Group involvement. You can go over the Ground Rules with each individual before the group forms, but it's even more important to go over them and discuss them together at your first meeting. You might even consider reviewing them, and asking, "How are we doing?" at the beginning of the other five meetings.

2. **Assign Working Partners** (Second meeting):

Working Partners will be assigned near the end of the second meeting. The Working Partner relationship takes the Achiever Group coaching concept one step further. The following three critical processes must be incorporated into the weekly activity of the partners to help each participant to truly break out of his or her comfort zone and accelerate achievement

- **Support** – Support must occur when it's needed most, not simply according to a pre-set meeting schedule.

- **Accountability** – Accountability for the daily activities and formation of new habits required to eventually achieve a future goal is what is necessary here, not accountability for achieving the goal sometime later. It takes 21 days to develop a new habit, and it's often tough to do it alone. In Working Partner relationships each participant becomes accountable to his or her partner for those activities and each partnership is in turn accountable to you, the coach-facilitator.

- **Feedback** – When working partners receive insight and suggestions regarding what they are doing effectively and what they can do to improve, from someone who cares (their partner), the helper role process is in action. Feedback creates a "grow as we go" experience.

Each working partner relationship needs to be documented using a *Working Partner Agreement* form. It is also helpful for working partners to use an *Activity Log* to record what is discussed when they meet, since they will be asked to report at the next Achiever Group meeting.

One of my favorite stories is about how working partner accountability led to one financial advisor landing his largest client. Here is how he told it.

It was Friday afternoon and I was cutting out early to watch my daughter's high school soccer game. I was already in the elevator when it dawned on me that I hadn't asked for a quality referral that day – which is one of my self-assigned fixed daily activities.

Well, since we had spiced up our working partnership by attaching a $15.00 bottle of Cabernet as a penalty for not completing all of your fixed daily activities during the week, there was no way I was going to deliver a bottle of wine to my working partner during our Monday meeting. As I rushed out of the elevator, I called one of my best clients and said something to the effect, "I've got this silly bet with a buddy in the office that I need to ask for one referral a day or else I owe him a bottle of wine. So, do you know anyone I should be talking to?"

In response, not only did his client not flinch at the approach, he amazingly replied, "I was just thinking about you – I'm glad you called because a good friend of mine just sold his business and was asking me for advice."

Would the client have called his financial advisor without the prompting stimulated by the working partnership accountability game? You never know. But that financial advisor is absolutely convinced that accountability to his working partner to do what needed to be done even when it wasn't convenient, was responsible for his acquiring his largest client. Sounds a lot like the common denominator of success doesn't it.

3. **Conduct an accountability update** (Second through sixth meetings):

The time frame covered by each update will be from the end of the last meeting to the beginning of the present meeting. Each update needs to be honest and up-to-the-minute.

To facilitate the process, it's important to provide an *Activity Log* to each group member at the end of each meeting. The log should provide space to write responses to the following questions each working day.

- What successes since the last meeting can you report, as a result of performing fixed daily activities?

- What difficulties did you encounter? What did you do about them?

- What have you learned from your experience with goal achievement, since the last meeting?

Kerry's confession regarding his fixed daily activities is a perfect example of how accountability updates can send you and the entire group, down an unexpected path. Kerry's peers did not anticipate his difficulties, but once he explained himself, everyone felt the freedom to be brutally honest and make the necessary changes to their own fixed daily activities.

4. **Present key concepts** (Every meeting):

One or more key concepts will be presented at each Achiever Group meeting, to help the group members understand what may be holding them back from becoming a high achiever. You will use the key concepts primarily as introductions to the group exercises.

5. **Facilitate group exercises** (Every meeting):

Group exercises are used throughout the six Achiever Group sessions. The purpose is to expand the participants' understanding of key concepts and help them to make a personal application of what they have learned. There will be a core exercise for each meeting as well as optional exercises you can use to expand the meeting.

Each exercise should include the following steps:

A. Explain the stated purpose for the exercise and review the steps they will go through, before they begin the exercise. Take the Holiday Inn approach – no surprises. It's a fact that people accept and do better with an exercise when they know why they are doing it and what to expect.

B. The next step is to do the exercise. Some exercises will be done individually; others will be worked on in groups of two or three. When two or more are involved, you may have them work with their working partner or you may have reasons to pair them with someone else.

C. The final step is to process the exercise with them, which involves asking a series of questions to have them explore the following three things.

What happened? – These questions will help them reflect on what they just experienced and collect their thoughts.

So what? – These questions will help them explore the meaning behind what they experienced, by asking them to dig deeper and form opinions about why it was a valuable experience and what they learned from it.

Now what? – These questions will challenge them to make a personal application and action decisions. This is the ultimate purpose of the exercise, to prompt action and move them toward achieving their goals.

Following are some **key concept/group exercise suggestions** for each of the six meetings, with the corresponding chapter where the material is presented shown in parentheses. Worksheets can be developed for any key concept or group exercise by using the corresponding material in the appropriate chapter. Examples will be described experientially in Chapter 14.

Meeting One

- Ground Rules – make copies to be distributed (Chapter 13).

- Goals and Motivation – McClelland and Atkinson Probability of Goal Success (Chapter 7).

- Quantum Growth Commitment – individual goal commitments.

- Fixed Daily Activities – individual action plans.

- Activity Log (Worksheet in Appendix).

Meeting Two

- The Achievement Cycle (Chapter 8).

- Pattern of Achievement (Chapter 8).

- Working Partner (Worksheet in Appendix).

Meeting Three

- Comfort Zone Expansion (Chapters 6, 7 and 8).

- Subconscious Mind (Chapter 6).

- Habits (Chapter 6).

Meeting Four

- Procrastination Avoidance.

- Procrastination Profile (Worksheet in Appendix).

Meeting Five

- Mind Power (Chapter 6).

- Constructive versus Destructive (Chapter 6).

Meeting Six

- Review.

- Individual Achievement Updates.

- Continuation of Achiever Group.

- New Quantum Growth Commitment.

- New Fixed Daily Activities.

- New Activity Log.

6. **Make assignments** (First through fifth meetings):

The following two assignments will be made as constants at the end of each Achiever Group meeting.

- Fill out your *Activity Log* – noting successes, difficulties, and things you learned, that you want to report at the next meeting.

- Schedule a Working Partner Meeting at least once a week – using the *Activity Log* to help plan and document each meeting (beginning with the second meeting).

As you approach the third meeting, you may be tempted to say something like, "By the way, don't forget your *Activity Log* and Working Partner Meetings." Resist that temptation by using the following techniques.

- When you make the *Activity Log* and Working Partner Meeting assignments, comment briefly on what you observed during the accountability update at the beginning of the meeting and provide feedback, starting with what was good about their reports and adding what could be improved. As you emphasize the continuous improvement, you will prevent them from becoming routine.

- If you make any additional assignments, explain the purpose of each and review the steps they need to go through, just as you would do when facilitating a group exercise. Make certain that the last step indicates how they are to report on this exercise during the Activities Check-Up time at the next meeting.

By the way, Kerry did not achieve the most success in his Achiever Group, although he did achieve his Quantum Growth Commitment. However Sam, another financial advisor in the group, assumed the leadership role by the fourth session when he established a second Quantum Growth Commitment after achieving his initial commitment.

Sam's story was revealed during the accountability update success stories and led participants to ask Sam questions about his success. His response was simple. "I made certain that I always completed my fixed daily activities every day, and I faithfully noted my progress and thoughts in my activity log."

Sam was a bit embarrassed by the attention, but from that point forward everyone in the group began keeping their *Activity Log* on a daily basis. They soon discovered that this simple daily task significantly improved their consistency to complete their fixed daily activities. They were basically using their *Activity Log* as a way to maintain accountability to themselves.

The learning that occurs in peer groups is a cooperative, active process of constructing knowledge.

BARBARA GLESNER FINES

As you can see, this is not complicated. But as you use this chapter as a guideline, keep in mind that whenever you are dealing with people, your common sense needs to be your ultimate guide. My objective as I worked with Kerry and Sam's group, even though it was a high-powered group, was to keep each participant engaged in his or her Achievement Cycle.

In Chapter 14, we will describe what the Achiever Group meeting looks and feels like. You will find that each of the processes will come alive when you can see them through the eyes of actual experience.

CHAPTER 14

THE ACHIEVER
GROUP EXPERIENCE

You miss 100% of the shots you never take.

WAYNE GRETZKY

The future isn't what it used to be.

YOGI BERRA

Although Achiever Groups come in many variations and almost every-one who strives to achieve could benefit from the experience, these groups are not just thrown together. A successful Achiever Group will be formed deliberately, with a common thread that ties the group members together and enables them to share similar experiences. The more group participants are able to identify with each other's efforts to achieve, the greater will be the impact of the group cohesion, modeling, helper role, and Achievement Cycle processes.

The Achiever Group meeting creates that common experience by re-viewing what *has already happened* and preparing for what *will* happen. It sounds simple, but without the accountability, feedback, and support necessary to focus and accelerate achievement, goals would not be achieved. Since achievement depends upon what is done rather than what is thought or felt, achievement is only an illusive dream when doing is absent.

The mission of the Achiever Group is to activate the Achievement Cycle in each participant and support each other's efforts to break out of their comfort zones and reach higher levels of achievement. Your task, as coach-facilitator, is to shape the Achiever Group experience for everyone, so let's take a look at what you could expect to experience.

PRIOR TO YOUR FIRST MEETING

We'll assume you have identified three people who absolutely must im-prove various aspects of their prospecting, qualifying, and closing skills and are close to a 'do or die' situation. You've decided that you need three to five more people to create just the right dynamics for a successful Achiever Group, particularly so that your Working Partners teams can be paired with two each. So, you begin your search.

After checking records and talking with some veterans, you identify three other people who could truly benefit from this particular Achiever Group experience. You then initiate conversations with each of the six people, making clear the benefits that they will receive and briefly reviewing the ground rules and types of activities they can expect to experience. When you know that they're set and you're set, you're ready to let the games begin! For the remainder of this chapter we're putting you in the position as the coach-facilitator, to help you see and feel the Achiever Group experience.

YOUR FIRST ACHIEVER GROUP MEETING

As you walk into the meeting room with a smile on your face, you're feeling positive about this new experience and hoping your smile will help to get everyone off to a positive beginning. Joining everyone at the round table that will help to facilitate interaction among group members, you notice that everyone is looking at you – probably wondering what will happen next.

You welcome everyone and review what each one can expect over the next 12 weeks, since you will be meeting every other week, making certain that you cover everything that you explained to the individual participants when you were recruiting them for the group. When you introduce the Achiever Group concept, you explain the importance of accountability, feedback, and support; and emphasize the need for ground rules.

Ground rules bring up the next task on your agenda. You hand out copies of the *Ground Rules* (Chapter 13) that you have printed on a single sheet and review them with a tone of finality in your voice, hoping they will understand the seriousness of the subject. But of course, one participant blurts out, "About this attending every session and not letting anything interfere; what if there's an emergency?"

You pause, moving your eyes around the group, and respond. "That's a valid question, but let's be honest. One person's emergency is another person's excuse. So, let me ask all of you – what kind of emergency other than a death, accident, or sudden serious illness, would you consider important enough to miss an Achiever Group meeting? Don't respond to me. Respond to each other." Although the ensuing conversation does not produce any dramatic conclusions, several of the participants stress that these meetings are too important to them for anyone to miss. The point has been made.

Acknowledging their honest, frank discussion you let them know that the next part of the meeting will give them more opportunities to participate fully in the Achiever Group experience. While introducing the Goals and Motivation *key concept* (Chapter 7) including McClelland and Atkinson's Probability of Goal Success, you can see heads nodding when you talk about the mistake of setting goals either too low or too high.

This is an important concept and it sets the stage for you to ask the group, "What does the phrase *Quantum Growth Commitment* mean to you?" To facilitate the conversation, you suggest first looking at each word and then putting the phrase back together. That really works, and everyone seems to realize that they are about to make a commitment and take a giant step forward in their profession.

They are now ready to complete the Quantum Growth Commitment exercise of determining what their goals will be and what steps they will take to achieve them.

- Each person writes down his or her goal on a blank sheet of paper.

- They then discuss and critique their goals, asking whether they are believable, achievable, and measurable. Some participants find they need to rewrite their goals.

- Next, they define and write down the specific fixed daily activities they must perform between now and the next Achiever Group meeting in two weeks, in order to make appropriate progress toward achieving their goals.

- Each person then signs and dates his or her Quantum Growth Commitment sheet.

You point out that the Quantum Growth Commitment is not directed toward the goal itself – but rather to the specific *activities* they need to do each day. That's the giant step they need to make – to not let anything keep them from doing what they have committed to doing. You hear someone comment that if the meetings are going to be this helpful, nothing will keep him away. You smile.

Ending the meeting with the distribution of the Activity Logs (see Appendix) to each participant, you explain that there will be an Accountability Update at the beginning of each meeting. You encourage them to use the logs to record successes, difficulties, and what they learn as they make the effort to complete the fixed daily activities on the lists they have just signed.

When you ask them for any final questions or comments, they thank you for your help, and you thank them for their cooperation and enthusiasm. As you collect all the Quantum Growth Commitments – you promise to make copies that will be distributed to everyone, and that you will return the originals.

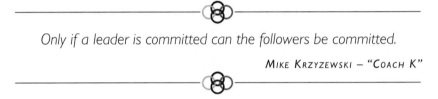

Only if a leader is committed can the followers be committed.

MIKE KRZYZEWSKI – "COACH K"

Your first Achiever Group meeting comes to a close; and as you leave the room you're thinking "A great start!".

BETWEEN THE FIRST AND SECOND MEETINGS

The next day you run off copies of the Quantum Growth Commitment signed sheets and deliver the copies and the originals as you visit each participant. During each visit, you talk with them about possible pairings for Working Partner teams, which you will form at the second meeting. It takes a couple of meetings with two of the participants, but you are able to firm up the pairings by the end of the first week. You also take the opportunity to remind each one that his or her Achiever Group success is more dependent on doing fixed daily activities than any other single factor.

YOUR SECOND ACHIEVER GROUP MEETING

As the group members arrive two weeks later, you immediately notice that their attention is directed toward each other (not you) as they find their places at the round table. That is progress.

Beginning with an Accountability Update, you ask each of them to report on any successes and/or difficulties they encountered while completing the fixed daily activities they assigned to themselves during the first meeting. Three participants admit they needed to fine-tune their lists later – and you congratulate them for doing that. Only one person reports getting through her list successfully each day. The others range from completing most of the activities most days to some of the activities some days. When you ask them what they need to work toward, beginning tomorrow, they respond in chorus, "All the activities all of the days!" You think, "Great! They're having fun."

Next, you ask them to think back to an achievement in their past that they are proud of accomplishing, revisiting their actions, thoughts and how they felt as they worked toward that achievement. You introduce the Pattern of Achievement concept (Chapter 8) and explain how this pattern is found in everyone, and then ask each one to write down the patterns of achievement for their accomplishments.

You then read them the following two story situations.

SITUATION 1

Tom has been a salesman for nine months. To meet his numbers, not to mention his own sales goals, he must improve his telephone prospecting habits and skills. He hates to make those calls asking for appointments. That's easy to understand; he's not very good at it.

Tom signs up for a one-day workshop on Telephone Prospecting with great expectations. He's right; the workshop is excellent. He leaves feeling like he knows what to do and how to do it. Because of all the role playing, he feels confident and eager to try his new skills.

The next morning, Tom wakes up to a cold and rainy day. "What a miserable day!" he mumbles to himself. "Boy do I feel lousy." Stumbling out of bed and grumbling through a light breakfast, Tom finally arrives at the office about 8:15 a.m. (In the workshop, he learned that he should be on the phone no later than 8 a.m.).

"I'm late already," thinks Tom. "There's no sense starting now. I'll just catch up on my paperwork. This evening I can review my workshop notes and be ready to start fresh in the morning." He turns his attention away from the telephone toward the pile of papers sitting in his In-Box.

SITUATION 2

Karen is an eight-year veteran stockbroker. She knows her business, but she has always struggled with the challenge of trying to manage multiple tasks and projects. Her understanding branch manager signs her up for a one-day Time Management workshop. Karen is very excited and grateful for the opportunity to learn how to "get things under control." Like Tom, Karen benefits greatly from the experience. One of the best parts is receiving a daily planner system. She learns that it will take about 30 days of concentrated effort to really learn and benefit from the system, so she makes a commitment to do exactly what is required. Karen knows that she will benefit from it.

The next morning, Karen too wakes up to a cold and rainy day. "What a miserable day," she groans. "But I am not going to let that deter me. I made a commitment to myself to begin that daily planner system this morning – and that's what I'm going to do. Right now!"

Karen bolts out of bed, fixes herself a cup of coffee, and begins. By the time she reaches the office, her system is set up. Her prospect and client management forms are filled out and stored in the proper place, and her tasks for the day are both listed and prioritized. She is concentrating so hard on what she's doing that she doesn't give the cold and rain another thought. When the day ends, Karen closes the cover of her daily planner system and says, "It sure feels good to be getting those projects and tasks under control!"

"What's the difference?" you ask the group. "Why was Karen able to do what she needed to do while Tom had such a difficult time and seemed to get stuck?" The conversation is lively, and several match their own experiences more with Tom than with Karen. You finally say, "Here's the answer" and walk them through the doing-thinking-feeling *Achievement Cycle* as described in Chapter 8.

"Which will it be for you?" you ask them. "The feeling-thinking-doing nonachievement cycle that enabled Tom to come up with an excuse not to do what he needed to do...or the doing-thinking-feeling Achievement Cycle that Karen embraced and resulted in positive thinking that produced good feelings?" The silence and serious looks on their faces speak loud and clear.

In the end, I always believe my eyes more than anything else.

WARREN BUFFET

After the brief pause, you continue, "When you find yourselves getting stuck, it's helpful to have someone right there to gently, or sometimes not so gently, push you back on your feet and get you moving ahead. In the Achiever Group experience, we call that person a Working Partner."

"After our first meeting, I met with each of you and discussed how we might pair you up into three Working Partner teams. We're now at a good point to formalize those pairings and begin the Working Partner process."

You have them pair off, and while they engage in some light conversation, you hand out the *Working Partner Agreement* forms (see Appendix) -- and give them about 30 seconds to look them over. Then you walk them through the steps.

- Each individual rewrites his or her Quantum Growth Commitment in the space provided on the agreement form.

- You then ask them to write down the fixed daily activities they need to complete between this meeting and the third meeting in two weeks.

- Finally, you ask them to share their Quantum Growth Commitment and fixed daily activities with their Working Partner, discussing the accountability, feedback, and support statements – and then sign and date the agreement form when they have finished.

As you distribute the *Activity Logs* to each participant, you remind them that you will again conduct an accountability update at the beginning of the next meeting. Before they leave, you instruct them to include their Working Partner meetings in their log and remind them that they are expected to meet at least once a week – and more often if they feel it would be beneficial. You suggest that they use these logs at those meetings to record what they discuss and any actions they agree to take.

As they leave, you point out that what they are learning here can be applied to other areas of their professional and personal life as well. The heads nodding in agreement confirm that this group is catching on. You all leave with good feelings about what is being experienced.

BETWEEN THE SECOND AND THIRD MEETINGS

As soon as you can, you find out when each Working Partner team will be meeting and then decide to wait until the second week to make a short visit to each. Two of the teams are working well. There is a high level of interaction between the partners with good accountability and feedback.

The other team appears to be *stuck.* "How are you doing with your fixed daily activities?" "OK," indicates a reluctance to open up. You suggest they ask more specific questions and give them a few examples to help them get started.

- What specific fixed daily activities are you performing as planned?

- What specific fixed daily activities are you finding it difficult to perform as planned?

- What seems to be blocking your progress?

- How can I help you and support your efforts?

As you leave the team, you can see that the questions are helping them open up, but one of the partners seems eager to make the accountability, feedback, and support principles work and the other partner is not cooperating. You decide to meet with the reluctant partner privately to see if you can figure out what's wrong.

When you meet with her, you find that she feels intimidated by her "more successful" (her words) working partner and is afraid she'll never measure up. You explain to her that growth and achievement are not about measuring up to someone else's performance, but are a series of day-by-day improvements.

You tell her that having a working partner who seems to do better than she at key tasks can be an advantage. The key is to develop the kind of working relationship where partners accept each other right where they are and are committed to helping the other do what they need to do to achieve their goal. You also tell her that she might be surprised at how much she can help her partner, even though she sees him now as "more successful," and that both of them have areas of strength as well as limitations that will provide ample opportunity for them to help each other.

After suggesting that you meet with the two of them again so that she can explain her concerns to her partner, and you can help the two of them discuss ways to make the experience a good one for both, she agrees.

When you meet, the encounter is a bit awkward at first, but the tension seems to ease as partners tell the other about their desire to make this work.

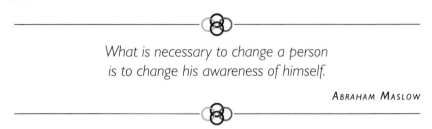

What is necessary to change a person
is to change his awareness of himself.

ABRAHAM MASLOW

All of your working partner teams are now communicating, and your Achiever Group is making progress.

YOUR THIRD ACHIEVER GROUP MEETING

As the group members arrive for the third meeting, you notice that the working partners naturally sit together and engage in friendly conversation as they wait for you to start the meeting. That's a good indication that the effort you made to help these teams gel is paying dividends.

During the accountability update, you sense more honesty as they report on their efforts to "do all of the activities every day." There are also a few *success stories* about how a working partner has helped his or her partner overcome specific obstacles. You are pleased to hear that, because it models to everyone what a working partnership should be – which is the value of having them share *success stories*.

You then ask if anyone has started applying the *Achievement Cycle* principle to any other area of his or her life. You see a few nods, but no one has anything specific to report. You tell them that you plan to keep asking that question at each meeting – because as they better understand the doing-thinking-feeling Achievement Cycle, you believe they will discover new and important ways of applying it.

Next, you introduce the key concept of Comfort Zone Expansion by saying, "All of us have formed our own comfort zone, and as long as we function within those parameters, we're feeling okay. But we are each now being challenged to achieve an important goal that requires us to break out of our comfort zone and apply the Achievement Cycle to activities that are not so easy or routine for us. To break out of that trap, we first need to understand how our comfort zone is formed and what it takes to break out of it."

You explain the *comfort zone* (reviewing Chapters 6, 7 and 8 which help you with the key concepts and exercises).

- How the subconscious mind operates (Chapter 6).

- How mental and doing habits are formed and stored in the subconscious mind (Chapter 6).

- How our comfort zone is shaped by those mental and doing habits (Chapter 8).

After facilitating a discussion on the key concepts, you ask everyone to participate in a 3-step exercise that will help them define their own comfort zone and begin the "breaking out" process.

STEP 1

Asking them to take out the list of fixed daily activities they created at the last meeting, you then suggest the following.

"It's likely that performing some of those FDAs has required you to go outside your comfort zone. It's also possible that some of the FDAs were left undone because of mental and doing habits that are blocking the way. Let's find out. Take an honest look at your typical pattern of daily activity and describe any thinking and/or doing habits that you believe are keeping you "locked" in your comfort zone."

After they make their individual lists, you ask each person to come up to the flip chart and first write down the thinking habits, and then the doing habits from their lists.

Under the thinking habits category, they list such things as:

- Thinking I have to learn how before I do it.

- Thinking of more important things I need to do.

- Thinking about the mistakes I might make.

- Rationalizing reasons to put it off until a later time.

The list of doing habits include:

- Doing daily routine things first.

- Accepting appointments and interruptions when I know I shouldn't.

- Wasting time until a meeting or appointment or something else comes up.

- Conveniently forgetting to do something.

    Note: If you needed to save time, you could have just had them write their lists at their seats and then share their lists verbally.

You are pleased with their self-awareness and honesty and move on to Step 2.

Step 2

Pointing out that if they find themselves locked into their comfort zone due to the habits they have listed, you suspect there are a number of fixed daily activities that are requiring that they "break the lock" so they will do all of those activities exactly when and how they need to be done.

You ask them to identify any specific fixed daily activities that require them to go outside their present comfort zone. You ask them to look over their list of FDAs and add any other activities that they have secretly kept off the list in order to avoid having to deal with them. You notice a few non-verbal "how did he know" type of reactions.

STEP 3

Telling them that breaking out of their comfort zone simply will not happen because they think it should, you ask them "What will it take?" They respond – "We need to **do it!**"

"You're correct, but there's more to it than that," you explain. "You also need to actively let go of those old habits you listed. You do that by forming new habits that will make doing those fixed daily activities part of your expanded comfort zone. They must be directly linked to the Quantum Growth Commitment you established at our first meeting, not just any old activity that makes you look busy. By getting rid of the old unproductive habits you will make room for the goal-directed activities."

Pointing to the flip chart, you explain: "These are the habits you need to let go of and replace. Think of it this way. You're standing here on the left. On the right are the fixed daily activities you are not presently doing like you should. In the middle is this first habit on the flip chart, 'Thinking I have to learn how before I do it.' In order to eliminate the gap, you need to get rid of the unproductive habit. You do that by replacing it with something else, like 'When faced with a new, uncomfortable activity, I will learn how to do it by trying it first. I will then evaluate what I did, make adjustments, and do it again. I will continue those four steps even when I believe I have mastered an activity.'"

You then ask the Working Partners to work together to write down new habits to be developed to replace every old thinking and doing habit on their list.

Chains of habit are too light to be felt
until they're too heavy to be broken.

WARREN BUFFET

After about 15 minutes, you bring the meeting to closure. Knowing that they have not completed their list of new habits, completing the list will be a vital part of the work they do with their Working Partner during the next two weeks. But you have one more reminder for them. The old habits they are trying to put aside are comfortable for them. The new habits are not.

So you ask them what needs to happen in order for them to "activate" those new habits. "We need to activate our Achievement Cycle," one group member responds. "That's right," you tell them. "When you meet during the next two weeks, make certain that you keep checking with each other to make certain no negative feelings or thoughts are getting in the way of doing what you have determined needs to be done. Remember, I'll be around to help you with that as well."

As they are about to leave, you remind them to use the *Activity Log* and include their Working Partner meetings over the next two weeks, emphasizing that two things need to happen during the next two weeks.

- First, they need to complete their list of new habits, making certain that each one is described well enough so that they know what that habit will look and feel like when they have mastered it.

- Second, they must begin developing those habits by actually using the habits to do each fixed daily activity exactly when it needs to be done.

You tell them that their *Activity Logs* can help them track their progress – and that this should be the primary focus of the accountability, feedback, and support processes at their Working Partner meetings.

As they leave, you're thinking, "A lot of stretching has taken place today."

BETWEEN THE THIRD AND FOURTH MEETINGS

A couple of group members contact you privately about the challenge it is to replace old habits with new ones. After listening to each one briefly, you encourage them to ask their Working Partner for help – promising to visit their meeting later and provide any additional help they might need at that point.

As you visit each Working Partner team, you find that some are having more difficulty than others – with putting old habits aside and with activating their Achievement Cycle when trying to focus on new fixed daily activities linked to their Quantum Growth Commitment. You remind them that this is how they will develop the new habits that they have determined are so important to their future success. As you focus on helping them help each other, you know that this interaction will be vital to their further growth when you are not around to encourage them.

YOUR FOURTH ACHIEVER GROUP MEETING

Expecting the accountability update to be livelier at the fourth meeting, you are not disappointed. Most of the group members have been able to complete their list of new habits, and several report some early progress in using those new habits to build their confidence when doing the most challenging fixed daily activities. You note those who are still stuck so that you can give them some individual attention later, knowing that the activities of this meeting and the next will continue to help all of them break out and move ahead.

During your most recent visits with the Working Partner teams, you observed several situations where efforts to hold each other accountable for new fixed daily activities were gratefully received and made a real contribution. In one case, they were asking each other how their new fixed daily activities would advance their efforts to achieve their Quantum Growth Commitment. Making that link was obviously very helpful to each of them, so you ask them to share their approach with the group as well as the *success stories* that resulted. It took a little extra time, but it was worth it.

When you ask if anyone has started applying the *Achievement Cycle* principle to any other area of their life, you realize that the "get rid of bad habits by replacing them with good habits" principle seems to have caught their attention. They have more to say about personal application this time, and much of it centers on bad habits they have committed to replacing with good ones. You are pleased!

What passes as common sense is often stupidity hardened into habit.

HERMAN WORK

Next, you introduce the key concept of Procrastination Avoidance saying, "At our last meeting, we focused on thinking and doing habits that tend to lock us into our comfort zone. You've identified what some of yours are and have started working on good habits to replace them. Today we want to look at one more habit – procrastination. Some of us struggle with it occasionally – others frequently. Regardless, procrastination blocks us from optimum achievement, so we need to do something about it."

Handing out the *Your Procrastination Profile* worksheet (see Appendix), you tell them that the 5-Minute Technique (as explained in the worksheet) really does work, and that they will find that it's even more effective after identifying the specific actions that cause them to delay getting started on the important fixed daily activities they have been working so hard to achieve. As they finish their Profiles, you check to make sure that they have each identified two or three areas of blockage that they are going to work on eliminating.

When everyone has finished, you ask if anyone has identified a specific blockage where the 5-Minute Technique will help. As they talk about their blockages, you ask what they are going to do to eliminate them, until you are satisfied that they have at least mentally prepared themselves to start putting the habit of procrastination behind them.

As you hand out the Activity Log for the next two weeks, you suggest that they focus on the following:

- First, they need to make good progress with letting go of their old habits and developing new ones. You remind them that psychologists say it takes about 21 days for a new behavior to become a true habit. You suggest they address this in their Working Partner meetings.

- Second, you remind them that they need to replace procrastination blockages with new behaviors like the 5-Minute Technique for the habit of procrastination avoidance. You suggest again that they make a real effort to help each other with this over the next two weeks.

Suddenly, an idea pops into your mind. You tell them that at the next meeting, you will be asking each group member to talk about the experiences they have with procrastination avoidance between now and when they meet. You suggest that they use their *Activity Logs* to record those procrastination incidents to help them remember what happened – and what they did about it.

You can tell as they leave that accountability is still a bit of a struggle for some of them so you try to think of ways you can make the next accountability update as positive an "accountability experience" as possible.

Between the Fourth and Fifth Meetings

The Working Partner meetings have been going well. But you know that they are all wrestling with letting old habits go as they make the effort to replace them with new ways of thinking and doing. You decide that a personal check-up with each group member would be beneficial at this point.

As you meet with each individual, you ask how he or she is doing – not in general, but specifically with his or her "habit replacement program." Each, in their own way, explains where they are in developing habits that keep them focused on doing what they need to do, in letting old habits go, and with breaking through any procrastination barriers that plague them.

Because of those meetings, you are better able to empathize with each individual's progress and you believe that everyone is making some progress toward achieving their goal. You note that two have been especially successful.

Your Fifth Achiever Group Meeting

Having met with each group member since the last group meeting, you expect that everyone will be ready to report on his or her "habit replacement and procrastination avoidance" efforts and success stories at the fifth meeting. You guess right. They are prepared, and although it takes longer this time, the accountability update goes well. Each person discovers that he or she is not the only one struggling with this transition and as a result, they begin to encourage each other and celebrate the small victories that other group members have experienced. You are really glad that you took the time to meet with each one over the past two weeks.

Before discussing this meeting's key concept, you tell them, "You probably thought we were done dealing with all the things that block us from doing what we need to do. Close, but there is one more. Today, we will be examining *Mind Power* and how destructive statements can lead to inappropriate behavior (Chapter 6). You then ask them to list three destructive statements and the opposite constructive statements.

You make reference to the "garbage in, garbage out" concept (negative thoughts and statements leading to negative feelings and behavior), making certain that it hits home, particularly for a couple individuals who you previously noted tend to react to things more negatively and cautiously than the others.

After the group members identify their personal lists of destructive statements and thoughts, you transform the concept of *Constructive Mind Power* into an exercise, instructing the participants to write at least one constructive "mind power" counter to a destructive thought or statement in their Activity Log every day.

Repeating the pattern you established at the end of the last meeting, you tell them that at the next meeting you will be asking each of them to talk about their experience with getting rid of the destructive mind power forces by using the action plan they just developed. Wishing them well, you hand out the Activity Log and again suggest that they use the log to record each occasion that they use any of the techniques, so they will be able to remember what happened – and what they did about it.

"We have one more meeting," you're thinking as they leave the room. "I want to be certain that they all receive maximum benefit from this Achiever Group experience. Maybe I should visit each individual again."

BETWEEN THE FIFTH AND SIXTH MEETINGS

After two check-ups, you discover that repeating the individual visit pattern probably is a good idea. You call the group members to schedule a visit with each one.

Everyone seems much more comfortable with applying what they learned about Constructive Mind Power at the last meeting. Following the same pattern for the fourth and fifth meetings has paid off.

You're thinking, "I'm ready for the last meeting – but what's more important, I believe they are as well."

YOUR SIXTH (AND LAST) ACHIEVER GROUP MEETING

Because this is the last meeting, you know that the group members could simply go through the motions knowing that "this is it!" But that's not what happens. As you go through the accountability update, each individual is eager to share and you find that they are very aware of the progress they have made – and quite honest about the remaining shortcomings.

Each individual has some of each, but what impresses you the most is each individual's obvious buy-in to their success, and their delight with what their Working Partner and other group members have achieved. It sounds and feels like an "achiever" group in the truest sense of the word.

When the Accountability Update is concluded, you express your sentiments about the group's progress. You tell them that your objective for this final session is to prepare them for life after the group, which will begin in about 30 minutes. You then hand them each a piece of paper and ask them to do the following:

- First, they evaluate their progress-to-date on the goal they originally brought to the group. Have they fully completed that goal? If so, you have them plan a specific way they will celebrate that fact. If not, you have them determine what remains to be accomplished – and define the specific fixed daily activities required to close the gap.

- Second, they create a list of goals that they should consider pursuing soon. You have them prioritize the list and select their top priority.

- Third, you have them establish a new *Quantum Growth Commitment* for their top priority. Using the same process you did at the first meeting, you have them define the specific fixed daily activities that they must perform in order to begin progressing toward achieving their new goals. You have them sign and date their new Quantum Growth Commitments.

- Finally, you guide them to determine how they will continue to work together – will they stay with the same working partners, keep meeting as a group, or possibly meet periodically over lunch?

As a final exercise, you ask them to write down on a piece of paper what they have learned during the past 12 weeks, that they believe will enable them to successfully achieve their future goals.

Finally, you go to the flip chart and ask them, one at a time, to tell you what they have written. You carefully write exactly what they say, tearing off and taping each flip chart sheet on the wall as it fills up. About six sheets later, they have finally given you what is the true value of the Achiever Group experience. It is not just a collection of what they were supposed to hear and remember. It is a list of how they have used what they learned and what they have discovered from that experience.

When the list has been completed, you tell them how proud you are of them and what they have achieved – and express your confidence that they will continue to achieve, even beyond what they have listed on their worksheet.

Most of the group members make personal comments to you as they shake your hand and leave. When you finally walk out the door, you're thinking: "This truly is as good as it gets!"

Although no two Achiever Group experiences are identical, there will always be a commonality when all of the sessions are facilitated properly and the "between meeting" work is taken seriously. My intent in walking you through a simulation of facilitating six Achiever Group meetings is to begin the process of experiential learning prior to your first real Achiever Group experience.

Note the "between meeting" coaching activities and the preparation such as reading chapters again in order to select key concepts and exercises. This behind the scenes work is what will enable you to maintain the momentum generated during the meetings and make the Achiever Group a true growth experience for you as well as your group members.

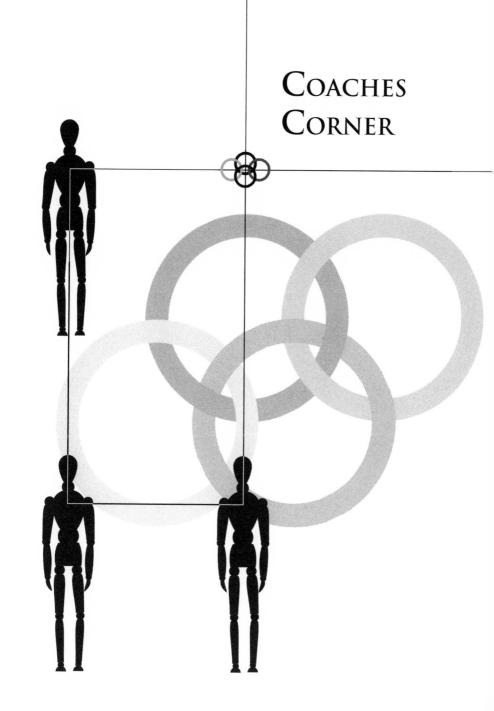

COACHES
CORNER

CHAPTER 15

THE TWELVE COMMANDMENTS OF FAST TRACK COACHING

Desire is the key to motivation, but it's the determination and commitment to an unrelenting pursuit of your goal - a commitment to excellence - that will enable you to attain the success you seek.

MARIO ANDRETTI

Do not let what you cannot do interfere with what you can do.

JOHN WOODEN

Your role as a FastTrack coach is to get people performing at higher levels than they would reach on their own, as you challenge them to change, to venture outside their comfort zones as they activate their achievement cycle. Your effective coaching enables the people you coach to break through what they may be thinking or feeling and do what needs to be done.

You are actually applying a principle of physics to human nature - The *Law of Inertia*, which tells us that *a body at rest will remain at rest until acted upon by an outside force*. A scientist might bristle at this simple definition, but it does provide some clarity to your role as a coach. It's clear that "acted upon" goes far beyond pat-on-the-back efforts to motivate or simplistic demands like "get on the phone and start calling people up."

Some say that coaching is no more than common sense, but I would call it uncommon sense, because very few managers understand the psychology of performance and the techniques for activating the achievement cycle. Now your new understanding can become part of your uncommon sense.

I have always been curious to discover how events in life are inextricably linked. Or at least I like to use my sense of curiosity to find a connection. A perfect example was an interview I heard on National Public Radio late one afternoon. A professor, whose expertise was in retail marketing, was being interviewed about K-Mart's recent filing for bankruptcy protection. I don't remember the exact wording of the NPR interviewer's question, but it addressed the issue of "What went wrong at K-Mart?" Waiting for a detailed response full of the latest business school jargon, I was surprised when the professor simply replied, "It can be boiled down to one word, Wal-Mart." Kudos to this unnamed professor. He could just as easily have given another one-name response – Sam Walton, Wal-Mart's founder.

Everyone is aware of Sam Walton's tremendous success, and we're reminded of it every time we enter a Wal-Mart store. But are you aware of his prowess as a hands-on coach? In Sam's autobiography, *Sam Walton:*

Made in America: My Story, Wal-Mart Vice Chairman A. L. Johnson explains Sam's style.

As famous as Sam is for being a great motivator – and he deserves even more credit than he's gotten for that – he is equally good at checking on the people he has motivated. You might call his style: management by looking over your shoulder.

A. L. JOHNSON

Raising expectations, motivating people to take action, and then holding them accountable for doing what they agreed to do, is the heart and soul of performance coaching. It's also on the list of Sam Walton's folksy business genius qualities. In his own way, he too understood that law of inertia. He knew that he had to put people into motion and make certain that they stayed in motion.

Keeping with the spirit of Sam Walton, I've decided to leave you with a simple, you might even call it folksy, set of coaching rules. I refer to them as the *12 Commandments of FastTrack Coaching,* another Baker's Dozen.

TWELVE COMMANDMENTS OF FASTTRACK COACHING
A BAKER'S DOZEN

COMMANDMENT ONE

Commit to performance improvement.

You cannot coach what you do not believe in your mind or do in your actions. As basic as this might appear, possessing a deep-seated commitment to improving performance is imperative to your success as a FastTrack coach.

Golfing great, Tiger Woods, is often cited for his success on the tour and his willingness to be coached. What is often overlooked is his personal commitment to improving, evidenced by the countless hours he spends after a tournament working on one aspect of his game that he is not pleased with. Some day he may be asked to coach others. If so, it will be his commitment to improvement even more than his skill as a player, that will make him a great coach.

In the words of Albert Gray, *successful people have developed the habit of doing what failures don't like to do.* As a coach you must believe, without proof, that performance can be improved and that stretch goals can be achieved. But before you can impart that commitment to others, they must observe it first in you. So as you look back over the past 30 days, are you performing at a higher level now than you were 30 days ago? If you are, did it happen by accident, or as an outgrowth of your commitment to improve? If you are not, how strong is your commitment to improve?

COMMANDMENT TWO

Be a leader – have and communicate a vision.

Remember Jerry in Chapter 2, the veteran manager with 70 financial advisors, who was able to get one of his top and most influential financial advisors into a coaching relationship? Jerry is a leader. Working behind the scenes, he was able to communicate his vision to a very successful financial advisor, someone prone to resist change. Change begins with having a vision for what the outcome will be.

Once that influential financial advisor got in motion, he agreed to enter into a coaching relationship. Jerry's vision and ability to communicate it became well known. Jerry conducted a meeting for all his financial advisors, articulated his vision, asked his big producer to say a few words, explained his criteria for entering into a coaching relationship, and suddenly had a line-up of people wanting to be coached. Jerry is now in the process of training his two assistant managers to become assistant Fast-Track coaches.

Commandment Three

Listen!

Sam Walton coached not only by looking over shoulders, but also by walking around and asking questions, "How could this be done better? What assistance do you need?" By asking the right questions and doing your homework on the people with whom you are entering into a coaching relationship, you will get a good working knowledge of their strengths and weaknesses.

That's what enabled me to quickly get Chuck's wealth management team back on track (Chapter 4). They were bragging about their new financial advisory process, but they were not bringing in enough new business. Although they had developed a complete metrics scorecard system, accountability was not in place.

As I listened carefully to all their reasons (excuses) for not bringing in enough new affluent clients, had I jumped in and started giving advice, I would not have discovered the real issue – Chuck. He was not setting the proper example. His weakness had always been prospecting, simply because he didn't like it. As soon as he committed to fixed daily activities that would get him face-to-face with affluent prospects and centers-of-influence, the rest of the team got in gear.

Commandment Four

Be selective – use the action agreement approach, but never assume.

I had a conversation with one of the top young managers at a major wirehouse who was being tapped for a major promotion because of his ability to coach performance. In my mind, he is also a terrific leader who can articulate his vision, change directions when appropriate, articulate the changes, and can coach people into the appropriate action.

In his words, *"Matt, I think we make all of this coaching much too complicated. Out of every 10 financial advisors in my complex, two are self-starters and easy to coach. Two are chronically plateaued and not likely to change. But it's the six in the middle where I'm able to get my greatest leverage as a coach. I think that's what sets me apart."*

Knowing this manager personally, I can assure you that it was not as simple as he makes it sound. Despite his success with his top two and middle six advisors, he did not simply ignore the other two. They had all been exposed to the FastTrack Coaching criteria and the five criteria for screening coaching candidates that we listed at the beginning of Chapter 3. He even initiated a coaching relationship with one of his chronically plateaued advisors, but when she failed to live up to her end of the first action agreement, he immediately terminated the coaching relationship. Selectivity without assumptions is essential.

COMMANDMENT FIVE

Set high expectations – be demanding.

No one has ever coached people to successfully attain higher levels of performance without being demanding. As coach, not only must you set higher expectations for them than they have for themselves, you must also hold people accountable to do what they need to do – and with enough force to get their attention. It's the old "inspect what you expect" philosophy.

This doesn't mean zero tolerance for failure, but it does mean zero tolerance for not doing what they agreed to do. You are coaching attitude and activities. When a financial advisor has committed to asking for one quality referral every day and is not doing so, if you buy-in to the excuse that "the market is down so everyone is upset, therefore the timing isn't right to ask for referrals" – you are neglecting your duties as a FastTrack coach.

Odds are that such an individual does not know how to ask for referrals, or may not have completed some of the process steps in building his 21st Century Financial Practice. Whatever the reason, a successful coach is demanding, does not accept excuses, and is always on the lookout for coaching opportunities.

Remember Linda back in Chapter 6? She presented a coaching challenge that was resolved by insisting that she focus on events she could control and stop bad-mouthing her firm and manager. Everything changed from that point forward. Expectations were created, demands were made, and performance was enhanced. This was simple in context, but not easy in application for either Linda or her manager/coach.

Commandment Six

Live and coach the achievement cycle – activity drives the dream.

Doing the right activity the right way for the right reasons on a consistent basis has always been the formula for success. This applies to the coach as well as the individuals being coached. Anyone can do what needs to be done when they "feel" like it. I have a neighbor who is terribly out of shape, but every once in awhile he gets the urge to take a walk. The problem he is facing when it comes to improving his overall health and fitness is that he's only taking walks when he feels like it. To live a lifestyle of health and fitness, he needs to be walking a set distance five or more days a week – even (or especially) on the days when he does not feel like it.

Let's take something simple like a coach's checkpoint/drop-in for example. As a manager/coach, you may be thinking that the visit is going to take more time than you feel you can afford, and that you have many other pressing matters. But as a successful FastTrack coach, you make the checkpoint/drop-in anyway. By doing what needs to be done even though you don't really feel like doing it, you are modeling the Achievement Cycle along with making certain that the individual keeps doing what he or she committed to do.

When you practice this on a personal level, it's much easier to coach people into their cycle of achievement. I often refer to it as "getting back in-play". I shared the case of Jerry back in Chapter 8 who was complaining about all the calls he was fielding from clients who had lost money owning Enron, allowing himself to feel their pain, and not doing the prospecting activities needed to continue building his business. Jerry was able to get back "in-play" by simply agreeing to do the necessary activities regardless of how he felt. When coaching is that direct, success is a direct result.

Keeping yourself and those you coach actively engaged in the Achievement Cycle is your common denominator for coaching success. Everything builds off of activity linked to a goal, including what I call the "business endorphin flow" created by the activity itself.

COMMANDMENT SEVEN

Search for and celebrate mini-successes.

No one major success is likely to take anyone you coach to the Promised Land. I know that stories abound about the "one" client that made somebody's career; but from a FastTrack coach's vantage point, those are merely stories. Rome was not built in a day and neither is a 21st Century Financial Practice. At a minimum, it's an 18-month journey that is going to have its share of ups and downs. Your job is to uncover and celebrate the ups while creating coaching opportunities out of the downs.

Since attracting the affluent is a new world for many financial advisors, mini-successes often take the form of setting upgrade appointments with key clients, getting a quality introduction from a powerful center-of-influence or being able to meet an affluent prospect face-to-face. When it comes to developing business with affluent prospects, the gestation period is often longer than many financial advisors are comfortable with. But as long as they are doing the right activities the right way, you want to keep their spirits up by looking for and celebrating even the small accomplishments that are building their confidence to produce greater accomplishments in the future.

COMMANDMENT EIGHT

Be involved – the right amount of face-time produces the best results.

Coaching is a contact sport. It requires rolling up your sleeves and mentally getting into the trenches with those you are coaching. Coaching is not the arena for ivory tower pronouncements. Simply being told what to do is rarely enough. Financial advisors also need to be shown how.

Beware of too much of a good thing. A firm I was consulting with created so much pre-work for their manager-turned-coach that the process became psychologically overwhelming and impractical for everyone involved. The initial coaching sessions were taking as much as five hours per financial advisor. Ouch!

Most coaching sessions should be no longer than 50 minutes. Why? It overloads those being coached. So how does a coach work toward getting the desired results? Weekly contact. You do not need to schedule weekly counseling sessions, but you may need to make daily checkpoint/drop-ins with many of the people you coach. Your formal quarterly review can be a scheduled event, but even then it should not last longer than one hour.

Commandment Nine

Control your ego – don't take credit for their success or own their failures.

I can remember experiencing both coaching success and failure within a two-day period. The failure was predictable. A particular financial advisor had sold me on his commitment to improve and develop a 21st Century Financial Practice. He completed all the pre-work to the satisfaction of my colleagues, but his problem became readily apparent when following-up with the first Action Agreement. The problem was basic; this individual was not doing what he had committed to do in the agreement, and he always had "good" reasons. It wasn't long before my office informed him not to be in contact until he fulfilled his initial commitments as outlined in the first Action Agreements. We have yet to hear from him.

The next day, I was to deliver a keynote address to a group of team leaders and was introduced by a manager who I had coached a number of years earlier. Much to my surprise, he insisted on giving me all the credit for the successes in his career. Comments such as these, as flattering as they might sound, make me uncomfortable – because they're not true. My role is only as a guide, showing people the way.

It is important to remember that achievement is the direct result of doing. That puts the full burden of responsibility on the individual. As a coach, we can only guide and encourage and push a little. That was my point as soon as I made it to the podium. Interestingly, not only did it make me more comfortable, it appeared to make everyone in the room more relaxed – including my introducer. I complimented him; after all he did the work. By taking myself off the false pedestal, my message became even more realistic for anyone interested in developing a 21st Century Financial Practice.

Keeping your ego out of coaching does not mean that your efforts will go unnoticed, or that your efforts had no influence. Results will always speak volumes. But you are a good coach if, and only if, the people you coach do what they need to do. The more a coach can control his or her ego, the better the results. It's a win-win.

COMMANDMENT TEN

Expand the comfort zone – yours and theirs.

One of the basic truisms in life is that if you are not going out of your comfort zone on a consistent basis, you are not learning and growing. If people are not learning and growing, they are not just stagnating; they are dying a little bit every day.

People tend to avoid what is uncomfortable, and more often than not it's this avoidance that disengages their Achievement Cycle. They stop doing activities that make them "feel" uncomfortable.

From a coaching perspective, the people with whom you enter into a coaching relationship usually know what they "should" do. That means they are consciously not doing it. The most common reason is that it falls outside their comfort zone. Consequently, you will only see results by helping them expand their comfort zone. The catch is that they will only expand their comfort zones by doing specific activities that make them uncomfortable. This critical relationship between the Achievement Cycle and their comfort zone is truly symbiotic.

By the way, as a FastTrack coach you too must do what makes you uncomfortable. Back in Chapter 2, Jerry went far outside his comfort zone to critique his top producer's business. If he had avoided making that stretch, the entire complexion of his coaching efforts would be different today.

COMMANDMENT ELEVEN

Be caring, but firm.

One of the areas we uncovered in a survey regarding branch managers was the importance that "caring" played in the context of being an indispensable manager. Caring was actually linked to personal issues such as physical health, personal health, family, and career.

The old saying, "I don't care how much you know until I know how much you care," is the heart and soul of coaching success. If someone gets the impression that you are only looking out for yourself, which is why it's important to control your ego, they may sabotage their own efforts for the simple reason that they do not trust your motives.

On the other hand, caring must not be at the expense of firmness. Bob, a team leader of a fairly successful group of financial advisors, had an assistant who had been working with him for 15 years. She was terrific, and he treated her like part of his family. As life often throws us unfortunate curves, the assistant's teenage daughter started running around with the wrong crowd and serious trouble followed.

Bob was helping at every step of the way, hiring the attorney, paying the fees, and truly being a caring boss. Unfortunately, all of this was at the expense of setting his daily business development appointments. And as you might guess, that was the one activity that pulled him outside of his comfort zone. Fortunately for Bob, his FastTrack coach gave him a week's grace period to deal with the problems and then became firm, insisting that he do his daily activities and not let the problems of his assistant become an excuse.

At first Bob was defensive, but he knew that his manager/coach also cared and reluctantly admitted that helping his assistant with her daughter's affairs did not have to interfere with his prospecting activities.

COMMANDMENT TWELVE

Insist on constructive mind power – avoid naysayers and eliminate excuses.

This is much easier said than done. Markets go up and down, clients are satisfied and dissatisfied, and change is a constant. On top of that is the fact that most people have developed the habit of focusing on problems rather than opportunities and solutions. In effect, every good coach quickly discovers that, left on their own, most people use their mind destructively more than constructively. In FastTrack Coaching parlance, they insidiously develop the self-limiting habit of destructive mind power.

A perfect example was Jim, a senior partner in a horizontal team composed of four financial advisors. His response to their 21st Century Financial Practice 5-year business plan was, "No way!" He then attempted to justify his negativity by explaining to his partners, "There is no way in the world we're going to have a billion dollars in assets under management within five years. Do the math. How much have we raised over the past five years? It's not even close."

As is often the case in these instances, Jim was absolutely correct. Individually and collectively, it took this group 20 years to raise the 350 million dollars they were currently managing. He was looking into the future from a historical perspective and his eyes were glued to the rear view mirror. However, his partners were committed to building a practice that would focus entirely on attracting, servicing and retaining affluent investors. From their vantage point, the future billion-dollar goal was doable, albeit a stretch. They had never been so focused before.

I was brought into all of this through a conference call arranged by their manager. After going over the business plan, metrics scorecards, and individual fixed daily activities, it was obvious that everyone was nervous. Deep down, the others were wondering if maybe Jim was right. My objective was to get them all using their minds constructively, which was accomplished in two simple steps.

I first took them to our 21st Century Financial Forecaster so they had it displayed on their screen. Second, I asked a simple question. "If everyone completed their fixed activities every working day of the year, using our Forecaster, what results could you expect over a 12 to 24 month period?"

I left them discussing whether they could raise 80 or 100 million dollars a year. Jim was still the skeptic, but now he has been forced to do his fixed daily activities and abstain from nay saying, or at least keep it to himself. As the mini-successes begin to accumulate, resulting from everyone doing their fixed daily activities, Jim's destructive thinking patterns will be replaced with constructive mind power. It happens every time.

COMMANDMENT THIRTEEN

Make it fun!

Life is too short not to have fun every step of the way. No one understood this better than Sam Walton. Each Saturday morning he would gather his associates together and lead the University of Arkansas Razorback cheer. Whenever he visited a Wal-Mart store he led another cheer with everyone spelling out W–A–L–M–A–R–T, one letter at a time, at the top of their lungs. In fact, he and his associates even performed this for President and First Lady George Bush, Sr. during their visit to Arkansas.

Think in terms of themes, creating a core culture and having contests that link the activities required to build a 21st Century Financial Practice: face-to-face meetings (present a mask to the weekly leader), money in the pipeline (Starbucks coffee mug to insinuate "plus $3.50 and you can get a latte."), net new money (Starbucks credit card, "now you can fill your mug.") and so on.

As a coach you must enjoy the process of challenging people to re-activate their achievement cycles, venture outside their comfort zones, and achieve at levels they would not reach on their own. Similarly, you are also responsible for making certain that everyone has as much fun as their personalities allow.

These three things - work, will, success - fill human existence. Will opens the door to success, both brilliant and happy. Work passes these doors, and at the end of the journey success comes in to crown one's efforts.

LOUIS PASTEUR

There you have it, another good-old Baker's Dozen. FastTrack Coaching is serious business that is best approached as a game that you play to win. You don't have time to tolerate fools or pretenders. You always make certain not to take yourself too seriously, since you must enjoy the game in order to excel.

Done properly, FastTrack Coaching can be one of the most exhilarating experiences of your career. But be careful, there's a good chance you might get hooked.

From one FastTrack coach to another – good coaching!

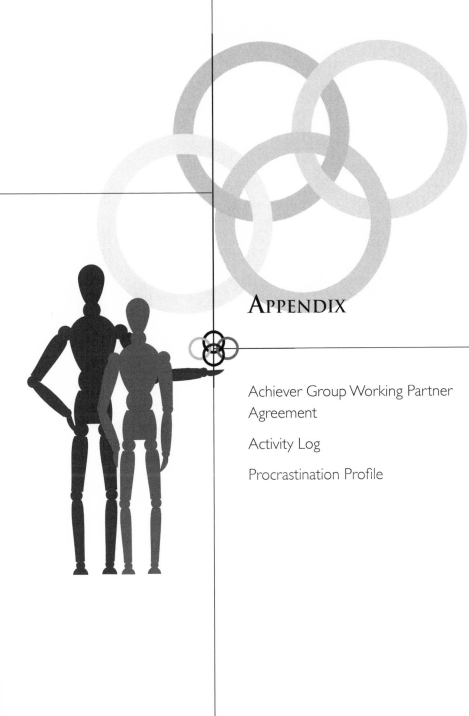

APPENDIX

Achiever Group Working Partner Agreement

Activity Log

Procrastination Profile

ACHIEVER GROUP
WORKING PARTNER AGREEMENT

This agreement is between/among the following Working Partners and is from the date shown below through the end of our Achiever Group Meeting 6.

Partner No. 1 _____

Partner No. 2 _____

Partner No. 3 _____

I, _____, have established the following **Quantum Growth Commitment**

```
┌─────────────────────────────────────────────────────────┐
│                                                         │
│                                                         │
│                                                         │
│                                                         │
│                                                         │
│                                                         │
│                                                         │
└─────────────────────────────────────────────────────────┘
```

To achieve that Commitment, I have identified the following **Fixed Daily Activities** that **I must do**.

1. _____

2. _____

3. _____

4. _____

5. _____

6. _____

To my working Partner(s):

• I am willing to be **held accountable** by you.   ___Yes ___No

• I am open to **receiving feedback** from you.   ___Yes ___No

• I am committed to **supporting you** by holding you   ___Yes ___No
  accountable and by giving you constructive feedback.

Signed _____   Date _____

Activity Log

Date	Time	Activity	Outcome Success or Difficulty	What I Learned

PROCRASTINATION PROFILE

For some people, procrastination is an occasional visitor; for others, it is a constant companion. In either case, it forms a blockage to goal achievement that can and must be conquered.

To help focus on the areas where procrastination may be a visitor or companion for you, circle YES or NO for each of the questions below.

1. Do you frequently put things off until the last minute?   YES   NO

2. Do you make excuses for unfinished work?   YES   NO

3. Do you avoid tasks that are unpleasant?   YES   NO

4. Do you have difficulty delegating tasks?   YES   NO

5. Do you find yourself challenged with managing your time?   YES   NO

For each of the questions you answered YES to, ask yourself one more question: Is this procrastination only an occasional visitor, or has it become a constant companion?

If procrastination is one of those "habits" you need to break, here is a technique that will work every time you find yourself putting an important activity on hold.

THE FIVE MINUTE TECHNIQUE

When you find yourself coming up with those excuses why you should not or do not want to *do it now*, do the following: 1) Take off your watch. 2) Commit to working on that activity for just 5 minutes. 3) Note the time and begin.

REFERENCES

Collins, James C. 2001. *Good to Great.* New York: HarperBusiness.

Dawes, Robyn M. 1988. *Rational Choice in an Uncertain World.* San Diego: Harcourt, Brace, Jovanovich.

Drucker, Peter F. 2001. *The Essential Drucker.* New York: HarperBusiness.

Drucker, Peter F. 2001. *Management Challenges for the 21st Century.* New York: HarperBusiness.

Fisher, Kimball. 2000. *Leading Self-Directed Work Teams: A Guide to Developing New Team Leadership Skills.* New York: McGraw-Hill Professional Publishing.

Fournies, Ferdinand F. 1999. *Why Employees Don't Do What They're Supposed To Do and What To Do About It.* 2nd ed. New York: McGraw-Hill Trade.

Hamel, Gary. 2000. *Leading The Revolution.* Boston: Harvard Business School Press.

Holiday, Micki, ed. 2001. *Coaching, Mentoring and Managing: Breakthrough Strategies to Solve Performance Problems and Build Winning Teams.* Franklin Lakes, New Jersey: Career Press.

Jackson, Philip. 1996. *Sacred Hoops,* New York: Hyperion Books.

Kinlaw, Dennis C. 1999. *Coaching for Commitment: Interpersonal Strategies for Obtaining Superior Performance from Individuals and Teams.* 2d ed. New York: Jossey-Bass.

Maraniss, David. 1999. *When Pride Still Mattered: A Life of Vince Lombardi.* New York: Simon & Schuster.

Secretan, Lance H. K. 1998. *Reclaiming Higher Ground: Building Organizations That Inspire Excellence.* New York: McGraw-Hill Professional Publishing.

About Matt Oechsli

Matt Oechsli is President of The Oechsli Institute, a firm specializing in servicing the financial services industry. For more than 20 years, he has coached financial advisors, teams, managers, and training departments to higher levels of effectiveness and success. He has also trained branch managers, industry trainers, and coaches on the art of performance coaching. This book has evolved out of those experiences.

Matt's *How to Build a 21st Century Financial Practice* has become the premier program for transforming transaction based financial advisors into solutions based financial practices and wealth management teams that are uniquely equipped to meet the multidimensional needs of the affluent.

Matt is an accomplished speaker, researcher, coach, and consultant. He has authored three best selling books, and his articles have been published in *Registered Representative* and numerous other financial services trade publications.

Matt lives in Greensboro, North Carolina with his wife and three children.